HOPE
AWAKENED

A workbook for people who have survived a suicide attempt and for those who have contemplated suicide.
Written by people who have survived, or have known the feeling of not wanting to live, and who are now thriving.

Trillium Center Inc.

Disclaimer

Nothing herein is intended to, or should serve as, a substitute for medical advice or diagnoses rendered to you by your individual doctor or other health care provider. Only a licensed physician should evaluate your situation, provide a diagnosis, or render other medical advice to you. Never disregard professional advice or delay in seeking it because of something you have read in this book. Medical treatment should be sought immediately upon the onset of symptoms, without regard to the content of this book.

If you are in crisis or you think you may have an emergency, call your doctor or 911 immediately.

If you are having suicidal thoughts, consider calling 1-800-273-TALK (8255) to talk to a skilled, trained counselor at a crisis center in your area at any time (National Suicide Prevention Lifeline). If you are located outside the United States, call your local emergency line immediately.

Trillium Center, Inc. is not liable for any action you may take based on information contained herein. Further, Trillium Center, Inc. is not liable for your reliance on any information published in any medium by any other institution or organization identified in any manner in this book.

Trillium Center Inc.

Authors	Editors	Illustrators
Trillium Center, Inc.	Cynthia Dudley	Risa Silver
Cynthia Dudley	Sharon Elliott Runge	Cynthia Dudley
Sharon Elliott Runge	Risa Silver	John Balano
Risa Silver	Michelle Zahn	
Michelle Zahn	Jill Wainner	**Cover & Layout**
Jill Wainner	Kevin Green	Cynthia Dudley
Kevin Green	German Gonzalez, Jr.	
Robert Johnson, III		
German Gonzalez, Jr.		
Brien Stewart		
Michael T. Lane		
Raymond T. Barnes		

Table of Contents

Foreword

Cynthia sharing her story in the opening of the book shows the courageous person she has become in her own journey, she is a million bucks and I am humbled and happy that our paths got to cross in my lifetime. To me, this is what living is all about, the experience of experiencing others through their journeys.

I was ten years old when I had my first suicidal thought. I was the number six child out of seven and a twin. My dad left earlier that year leaving my mom to raise us on her own and I did not make that any easier on her. I wasn't her favorite because I reminded her of Dad, which meant I pretty much always got the short end of everything, including attention. So later that year, I truly believed that the world would be a better place without me.

Similar to Cynthia's story, I decided to dream differently and create new habits that would show me new opportunities in life. I told myself that if I could live to see 50 years of age, I would remember this day and the conversation I had with myself about living my life to it's fullest. I carry a picture of my 10 year old self with me every day and have a conversation with "Sean" (that's what my friends and family called me growing up) and he tells me every day how proud he is of the man we've become.

This book will help so many people get through their darkest days.
Will it be easy?
No.
Will it be worth it?
Like the Trillium Team has said…. ABSOLUTELY!

Victor S. Angry
Neabsco District Supervisor, Prince William County Board of County Supervisors
Former Command Sergeant Major of the Army National Guard (retired)

Acknowledgements

This book truly has been a labor of love.

It has taken many months and a lot of edits. Here we have it completed: **Hope Awakened: A workbook for people who have survived a suicide attempt and for those who have contemplated suicide. Written by people who have survived, or have known the feeling of not wanting to live, and who are now thriving.**

We have compiled some great information and created awesome worksheets that would have been a huge help for some of us during our darkest days. Some of us have had more suicide attempts than we can count, and many more days of merely wishing to not be alive because the psychological pain was so great. Some of us, while not having attempted suicide, have known the feeling of not wanting to live anymore or wanting the pain to end. All contributors have an endless amount of empathy. They all work with others to support them through their journey.

Of course we could not have covered every single element that propelled us into the successful lives we live today. But we are confident that with progress in one area of our lives, other areas will improve, also. It is a natural process, a process in which we have faith.

The information contained in this book was created by us, people who have lived experience of mental illness. We are not clinicians, therapists, psychologists or psychiatrists. We did not consult professional research studies. We are people who have gone through the process and have been working in mental health peer support for a number of years. Three of us since 2007, for over 14 years. Many of us are certified PRS by the Commonwealth of Virginia and have helped thousands of people in our community in their mental health recovery. We are committed to the work we do and always look for ways to help even more people. To us, it matters.

There were many people that worked on this compilation: Cynthia Dudley, Sharon Runge, Risa Silver, Michelle Zahn, Kevin Green, Robert Johnson, Jill Wainner, and German Gonzalez. They are The Trillium Team. They all put their hearts into the material to make sure we were getting it right from a group perspective.

This Team is led by Cynthia, the Director of Trillium Center. The Trillium Team have been together for lots of years and she could not be more proud of the people they have become just in the time she has known them. In those quiet moments when she reflects on each of them individually and holds it all in her heart she can feel tears touch her eyes in a glimmer of their sheer beauty. She is proud and oh so lucky they are all a piece of the puzzle that creates recovery oriented services for our community.

We also reached out to other leaders in the peer support world. Michael Lane, Brien Stewart and Raymond T. Barnes all work in Virginia at various positions in our profession that serve others with mental health challenges. They all have carved their own paths in the world and impress us greatly.

We are always grateful to our Board Members: Geri Weeks, Dennis Hunt and Shannon Shy, for their encouragement and unconditional support for all we do.
Our funding sources, Prince William County and Potomac Health Foundation have been quite supportive of the work we do in our community. Their belief in Trillium Center has been amazing over the years and we are eternally grateful.

Supervisor Victor Angry was a blessing for us in this project. His encouragement is amazing, his review of our work and kind words in his Foreword touched us deeply, and we could not be more grateful.

We owe a debt of gratitude to Victoria Graham, who, for 30 years, managed our community crisis line. Vicki read our draft copy and offered much support and insight to the team. Years ago she reached out to partner with us on a monthly support group for suicide attempt survivors called Renewed Hope. Vicki offered a booklet to go along with the group, which was a compilation of pages collected from various sources. That booklet provided stimulation for some of the work we created in **Hope Awakened**. It also inspired us in ways we could not have ever imagined. We adore Vicki who has dedicated her life to be in service to others.

BEYOND
GRATEFUL

We are super grateful to Rita Romano, Tom Geib and Ann Brown. Who have dedicated their lives to serving people with mental health challenges. All three have had strong connections with Trillium since before we opened our doors. They were meticulous in looking over our work and providing much needed input to give our readers a clearer picture. Their words inspired us to dig a little deeper and create pages that are even more helpful. We appreciate all three of them so darn much.

Canva has been one of our creative tools to create this workbook. We have much gratitude to the application and to the artists who have contributed their work for us to use.

Michelle Zahn is the person who lit the spark to create the flame that became our passion to develop this workbook. She deserves a super duper dose of gratitude in this process.

Our acknowledgement page would not be complete without recognition of our intrepid leader, Cynthia Dudley. It seemed she always understood what needed to go into this workbook. She is our leader, our organizer, and none of this would have come to fruition without her.

We have to mention the person who initially had the vision in the work we do on a daily basis, Ann Gurtler. Way back in 2007 she had the dream of serving people living with mental illness in our community. She knew from experience how isolating it can be and how stigmatizing mental illness is. Trillium would not exist without her commitment and vision. We know she is looking down from above and cheering us on, as only Ann could do.

We are quite proud of **Hope Awakened**. We hope you find some helpful information in this book that will assist you on your journey. We are so grateful to be alive ourselves, and hope this book inspires others to find their way out of the darkness of suicidal thoughts, feelings and actions.

The Trillium Team

About This Book

This is a book written by people who have lived experience of suicide attempts and by others who, while not having attempted suicide, have felt the feeling of not wanting to live anymore or wanting the pain to end. While it may be in line with some research studies, it is based entirely on what has worked for us. We have been using earlier versions of this book in support groups.

Your life is your work. It is not "someone please fix me." It took some of us a long time to learn that. We hope in the pages of this book, that you will get that particular message loud and clear. It is all about you. Your choices, your definitions, your work. Your life.

Complete this book with a friend, family member, therapist or a supportive person in your life. Or complete it on your own, if you so choose. Some folks that contributed to this book thought support might be critical. Others thought they would prefer to do it on their own.

If something does not resonate in this book with you in one reading, feel free to skip it and keep going. We strongly encourage revisiting the skipped section at another time or many times if needed.

All of the worksheets included in this book can be reprinted as much as you would like. You can find the worksheets and other printable documents here:

https://TrilliumCenterInc.org/HopeAwakened.php

Hello there

Thanks for looking at this book. I am proud of you.

I lead the team who put this book together. We have been working on it awhile and found it was ready to share with you.

During the compilation of exercises, it occurred to me how scary a book like this might have been for the person I used to be.

As I sit here and breathe, I am wondering what part of my story would be most helpful. The most important thing to say is: You Matter. I do not know you, but I know from the bottom of my heart with all of my being that _You Matter_.

During my darkest days, which lasted for YEARS, I didn't feel like I mattered. Heck, I didn't feel human. The worthlessness I felt was all encompassing and my life was empty. I had taken my distance from my family and had trouble keeping friends and couldn't hold a job for very long. My life felt totally empty, and quite honestly, pathetic.

After too many suicide attempts toward the end of my dark days, for the first time I checked myself into a mental health hospital. For fourteen years I had been working with a psychologist diligently on my early childhood trauma. I was 5 when I had my first attempt. I was 12 when I realized just how messed up my thoughts were and that it was going to take a long time to work it out and feel some kind of 'normal.'

During my hospital stay, at 38, some switch flipped inside me. Right in one moment, I realized I had become the woman I had been fighting to be.

And decided to not look back. I was certainly 'good enough.' At 56 I still haven't looked back. Occasionally a memory will creep up to try to distract me, but one of the most important things I learned was *I* get to choose what *I* think about. I don't have to follow every thought that pops into my head. I couldn't anyway. I have a lot of darn thoughts. Knowing I can pick and choose, though, feels quite empowering. And, between me and me, letting a thought pass me by clearly lets ME know *I* am in charge of *ME*.

I GET TO **CHOOSE** WHAT *I* THINK ABOUT.

There were so many years filled with not much. My life certainly felt overwhelming, unmanageable, and completely empty. As I look at it now and think about that moment in the mental health hospital; there was an internal shift in focus. I began to look at life better. It sounds corny, but almost overnight I looked at life as a glass half full. Even though I still had nothing, really. Still no family, still no friends, still no job. But internally, *I* had changed. Somehow all the pieces fell into place and I realized *I* could see MY world differently!

In hindsight, it seems similar to making a new habit. I decided in a moment to make a new habit about how I choose to see my life.

Now, so many years later, my glass is definitely overflowing.

I created my own career path and now I get to help a lot of people on their mental health recovery journey. I've won some professional awards and have made a place for myself in our community. I think about how far I have come and I feel this blessing come over myself and am in awe. I wish I had known then what I know now. I am grateful every single day that I am alive.

My team understands the struggle. All of us. We all work so hard to do what we can to help people understand that mental health recovery is possible. Not only is it possible, but we believe everyone can achieve it.

You deserve a beautiful life.

We do not know you, but we are here cheering you on. Hold on tight and borrow our strength if you need to. We have a LOT to share.

Your mental health recovery is between you and you. No one can do it for you. No one can tell you how to do it. People can support you. We are here to support you through the pages of this workbook. Your path is unique and all about you. The way through the pain and into mental health recovery is within you.

We have created this workbook to help you as best we can. Most of the exercises are ones that most of my team and I have done. Sometimes more than once. Sometimes a lot. Just know we are here. And we believe you can do it.

Sending you peace, strength and courage,
Cynthia

Just a reminder in case your mind is
playing tricks on you today:

You matter.
You are important.
You are loved.

And your presence on this
earth makes a difference
whether you see it or not.

Trillium Center Inc.

Everyday Victories

For Someone Living With Mental Illness

Simply getting out of bed. ✿ Exiting the comfort and safety of my home. ✿ Braving the outside world. ✿ Setting an appointment. ✿ Making a conscious effort to go out and have a good time. ✿ Going for a nice, quiet walk by myself. ✿ Meeting up with friends. ✿ Not feeling like an unnecessary presence. ✿ Achieving a personal goal I've set for myself. ✿ Recognizing that I've achieved something. ✿ Congratulating myself on doing something. ✿ Being flexible as a situation changes. ✿ Not over thinking any vague comment, online or real world. ✿ Overcoming the terrifying task of answering a phone call. ✿ Making a phone call. ✿ Making a phone call to a stranger. ✿ Making any future plans. ✿ Sticking to plans. ✿ Completing something I've been putting off for a long time. ✿ Making a decision within a sensible time frame. ✿ Not second -guessing a decision. ✿ Being the one to actually initiate a conversation with a friend or colleague, instead of expecting them to. ✿ Joining an ongoing conversation without being asked a direct question. ✿ Not feeling like a burden. ✿ Not starting every other sentence with the word "sorry". ✿ Responding to a compliment by simply saying "thank you". ✿ Going a whole day without relying on self- deprecating humor. ✿ Going a whole day without unnecessarily criticizing myself. ✿ Making small talk. ✿ Dancing with or without someone else. ✿ Applying for a job, getting a job, working. ✿ Doing something I enjoy even if it takes a lot of effort. ✿ Having "ME" time. ✿ Spending time in nature. ✿ Doing something fun. ✿ Smiling. ✿ Staying positive. ✿ Going somewhere new. ✿ Surviving an elevator ride. ✿ Speaking during a meeting when I have something to say. ✿ Receiving an email with a scary sounding subject and, instead of ignoring it, reading it immediately. ✿ Not worrying about getting fired from my job. ✿ Completing something that's challenging. ✿ Doing something that's physically active. ✿ Sticking with something that's difficult. ✿ Finding hobbies I enjoy. ✿ Making time for favorite hobbies. ✿ Eating healthy. ✿ Drinking enough water. ✿ Going on a special trip. ✿ Completing daily self-care routine. ✿ Going somewhere I've been before. ✿ Socializing with friends. ✿ Meeting new people. ✿ Having a question and actually asking it. ✿ Needing help and actually asking for it. ✿ Falling asleep within one hour of going to bed. ✿ Not going over every little perceived mistake I make throughout the day. ✿ Making it through another day. ✿ Laughing. ✿ Appreciating what's good about my health ✿ Feeling valuable ✿ Creating or maintaining a friendship ✿ Giving myself credit for everything I've achieved during the day. ✿ Doing something special just for me. ✿

Trillium Center Inc.

Prevention

Reasons for Living

These are reasons why some people have chosen to live after experiencing suicidal thoughts or an attempt. Please look over the list and check <u>all</u> the statements that may be true for you.

	Learning to manage my problems is something I can and am willing to do.
	My life and destiny are truly under my control.
	Uncomfortable feelings do not last.
	Things may change for the better.
	It may seem like I am alone, but there is help available if I reach out for it.
	Many thoughts and feelings that I have may be unreliable.
	People care even if they do not always know how to show it.
	Difficult thoughts do pass.
	Feelings are not permanent.
	I am stronger than I realize at this moment.
	My family might believe I did not love them enough to fight to stay alive.
	I do not want to hurt my loved ones.
	I want to watch my children/or others' children as they grow.
	I could not leave my family whom I love.
	The effect on my children could be harmful.
	What others think is a concern to me.
	I believe killing myself would not really accomplish or solve anything.
	I would not want my family to feel guilty afterwards.
	Thinking about the act of killing myself is scary.
	I can find a stable place again.
	I can accept responsibility to manage my life.

	I can develop meaning and a desire to live.
	I am open to finding other solutions to my problems.
	I am able to dream and create a better future for myself.
	As I progress in my recovery, I can help others who are struggling.
	I can develop courage and resilience.
	Suicide is opposed to my spiritual path.
	There is beauty in life and I can learn to focus on that.
	I do not know for certain what the consequences of suicide are.
	I do not want to make people who care about me suffer.
	I do not want to die.
	I have a desire to live.
	There is a beautiful and fulfilling life for me just around the corner. I just cannot see it yet.
	I want to experience all that life has to offer and there are many experiences I have not had yet which I want to have.
	I make a contribution to society.
	I am curious about what will happen in the future.
	My life has meaning.
	I am here for a reason.
	I am part of a greater good.
	Who will take care of my dog or pet?

Other reasons for living:

_____

_____

Other reasons for living (con't.):

_____

_____

_____

_____

_____

_____

Now look over the list and the items you have added.
Which are your top three favorite reasons for living?

_____

_____

_____

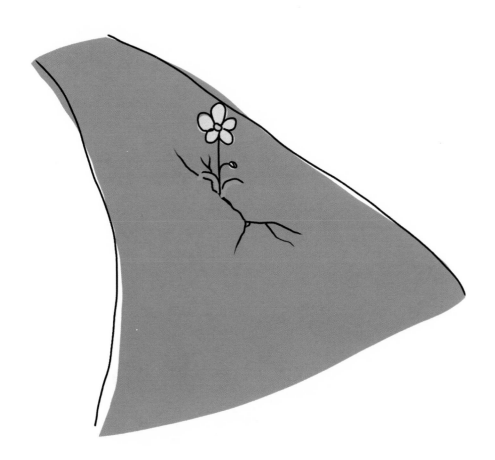

Foundation to
Mental Health Recovery

Many of us in mental health recovery have tools we rely on to continue on our path of wellness. The following list is what we all most have in common. Take a look at this list and see how it works for you. Add your own tools for your recovery at the end of the table.

Item	Benefits me currently	Needs work	Doesn't interest me	More thoughts
Daily Structure				
Exercise				
Family				
Friends				
Primary Care Physician				
Living Situation				
Medication				
Meditation				
Nature				
Nutrition				
Peer Support				
Pets				
Psychiatrist				
Sleep & Rest				

Item	Benefits me currently	Needs work	Doesn't interest me	More thoughts
Supplements				
Spiritual/Religious				
Support Groups				
Support Network				
Therapist				
Vitamins				
Volunteering				
Work				

Possible Warning Signs

In order to learn how to prevent a crisis, some people find it helpful to understand what they feel prior to a crisis. While many of these items may come up in everyday life that are unrelated to a crisis, they could become a warning sign. Which of these do you experience before a crisis begins?

Circle all that apply.

- Mood
    - Feeling like things will never get better or nothing will ever change
    - Feeling overwhelming guilt or self-hatred
    - Depressive mood
    - Severe anger or irritability
    - Feeling powerless
    - Feelings of helplessness or hopelessness
    - Lack of interest in hobbies and/or activities
    - Feeling worried or overwhelmed
    - Loss of self confidence
    - Feeling worthless or shameful

- Behavior
    - Talking about or feeling anxious, sad or bored
    - Pacing or inability to sit still
    - Behaving recklessly
    - Using substances to self-medicate
    - Too much or not enough sleep
    - Neglecting personal appearance, hygiene and responsibilities
    - Eating less, severe dieting, or eating more
    - Getting in trouble, being aggressive or rebellious
    - Compulsive or impulsive behavior
    - Withdrawing from friends or family
    - Talking or writing about suicide or death
    - Cutting oneself
    - Having low or no energy

- Thought
    - Nothing to look forward to
    - Poor judgment
    - Confusion
    - Exposure to triggering events, places or people
    - Inability to concentrate or focus
    - Loss of concentration in school, work or routine tasks
    - Difficulty making decisions
    - Thinking of hurting or killing yourself or someone else

Trigger Tracker

Trillium Center Inc.

Understanding what occurs before a mental health crisis can be super important to preventing future crises. Use this form to help you understand what can precipitate a crisis. Please make copies of this sheet as you need them.

Date: _____ Time: _____	Date: _____ Time: _____	Date: _____ Time: _____
Activities before being triggered	**Activities before being triggered**	**Activities before being triggered**
• • • • • •	• • • • • •	• • • • • •
Symptoms I am having now	**Symptoms I am having now**	**Symptoms I am having now**
• • • • • •	• • • • • •	• • • • • •
What I can change in the future	**What I can change in the future**	**What I can change in the future**
• • • • •	• • • • •	• • • • •

These are things that work for some people. Circle ones that may work for you.

- Create structure for each day
- Get enough sleep
- Connect with other people every day
- Take medications as prescribed
- Have a stuffed animal or pillow to hug
- Have healthy ways to relieve stress
- Think clearly as possible
- Go to all medical appointments
- Go outside to spend time in nature
- Have healthy ways to express anger
- Use a journal to get emotions expressed and out
- Eat something healthy
- Give others my full attention
- Talk with doctor about vitamins and supplements that can help my mental health
- Find reasons to laugh
- Maintain healthy relationships
- Use positive self-talk
- Attend support groups regularly
- Express feelings to others in a healthy way
- Take a bath or shower
- Plan fun activities for myself
- Learn how to set and maintain healthy boundaries
- Exercise – go for a walk
- Listen to others
- Leave the area in times of conflict with others
- Gardening
- Breathe deeply
- Call a friend
- Help someone else
- Listen to music that soothes you
- Watch a movie, especially a comedy
- Read
- Write, paint, draw, sing, play music
- Care for an animal
- Express gratitude
- Find something to look forward to
- Follow your **Self Care Plan (see page 93)**

For me, having things to look forward to helps me avoid going into crisis mode. Sometimes, I can appreciate the thought of something big that may be on the horizon. Other times, I have to find something small to set my sights on. Either way - whether it's just a new season coming up, or my daughter's wedding - I think about it frequently and appreciate that it's there to look forward to. - Jill

When my thoughts start moving fast it feels like that world globe in school where people would spin it and spin it as fast as they could. I know at that point I need to unplug. Turn off the tv, turn off my phone. Close down all other electronics and put myself in bed. Just shut down and rest until the racing thoughts subside. - Robert

Exercises that May Help

Centering, or grounding exercises have been useful to some people. Try these exercises when experiencing anxiety, a crisis, or dissociation to center or ground yourself.

Five senses
Engage all your senses:
- 5 things you can see
- 4 things you can touch
- 3 things you can hear
- 2 things you can smell
- 1 thing you can taste

4-7-8 Breathing
Breathe in for 4 counts
Hold breath for 7 counts
Breathe out for 8 counts
Repeat 5 times then take a break

Food
Take a nibble of a food you enjoy. Savor it. Notice the texture and all the subtle flavors. Crunchy? Smooth? Rich? Mellow? Salty, sweet or sour? Etc.

Memory game
Focus your attention on your surroundings. Try to memorize everything you can see. Close your eyes and recreate the scene. Open your eyes and compare. What did you remember? What did you forget?
This is not a contest, just a way to connect with your physical surroundings.

Breath
Sit comfortably, but not slouched. Rest your awareness on your breath. Notice what it feels like going in through your nose. Feel your ribcage and abdomen expand. Notice the pause between the in-breath and the out-breath. Notice the sensation of your ribcage and abdomen contracting. Be aware of what the air passing out through your nose feels like. Notice the pause between the-out breath and the in-breath.

Distraction
Take your mind off the problem for a while. Puzzles, books, artwork, crafts, knitting, sewing, positive websites, music, movies, do something special for someone else, exercise, look through old pictures, talk with a friend, dance, scribble, play basketball or other games, write poetry, take up a new hobby.

Health & Hygiene
Take care of yourself. Eat well, exercise, shower, do laundry, household chores, hydrate, rest, take vitamins, medications, wear something that makes you feel great, paint your nails, make hot chocolate or a smoothie, try to do handstands or cartwheels, play soccer or frisbee with a friend.

Emotional Awareness
Tools for identifying and expressing your feelings. Use a list or chart of emotions, write in a journal to explore how you feel, type about how you feel while listening to music and not thinking much, use a mood-tracker, draw, paint, let yourself cry, pray, hug a pillow or stuffed animal.

Walk in the Grass
Find a grassy area like your yard or a park. Take off your shoes. Walk around barefoot. Focus on the grass and ground under your feet.

Connect with Reality
Tools for centering and grounding yourself in the present moment. Mindfulness, meditation or relaxation, grounding objects like a rock or paperweight, yoga, breathing exercises, talk with a friend, focusing, exercise, perform a random act of kindness.

HALT
Do not allow yourself to get too **H**ungry, **A**ngry, **L**onely or **T**ired.
Check in with yourself. Are you hungry? Eat something. Angry? Write out what's going on, if there's constructive action you can take, do so. Otherwise, let it go. Lonely? Call a friend or a warmline. Tired? Lay down and rest or take a nap.

Opposite Action
Doing something the opposite of your impulse that's consistent with a more positive emotion
1. Affirmation & Inspiration - looking at or drawing motivational statements or images
2. Something funny or cheering - funny movies, tv, books, a friend
3. Use gratitude - make a gratitude list
4. Make a list of your accomplishments, even something simple, like getting out of bed

Coping Skills

Everyone uses coping skills. They can help you when you are feeling stressed, upset, angry, etc. Coping skills can be tools to use to change your focus, at least for a little while. You can use these suggested activities to try when thoughts come up about hurting yourself in order to change your focus. Add some other things under each category that may help you while in a crisis.

Physical Space
- Declutter
- Alphabetize movies and books
- Clean your house
- _____
- _____
- _____

Physical Activity
- Go for a run
- Do Tai Chi
- Dance
- _____
- _____
- _____

Nature & Outdoors
- Plant seeds to grow
- Go on a hike
- Do yardwork
- _____
- _____
- _____

Hobbies & Crafts
- Paint or draw
- Knit/crochet
- Do a crossword puzzle
- _____
- _____
- _____

Entertainment
- Go to a theatre
- Watch your favorite shows
- Play board games with a friend
- _____
- _____
- _____

Pampering
- Get your hair done
- Burn incense
- Get a massage
- _____
- _____
- _____

Animals
- Play with a pet
- Go bird watching
- Volunteer for an animal shelter
- _____
- _____
- _____

Fun & Miscellaneous
- Start a collection
- Blow bubbles
- Collect positive sayings
- _____
- _____
- _____

I find that a bath is very soothing. It helps me manage anxiety by allowing me to calm down in the warmth of the water. When I'm more relaxed, I imagine that all the negative thoughts and feelings have washed away, and I watch them go down the drain. - Jill

When I am starting to dissociate, one thing that can both soothe and help me get grounded again is to count coins. I can put a whole jug of coins on a bed or on the floor and just count. There is probably some science behind this action but I simply know it works for me. - Cynthia

Ann lived by HALT. She simply would not allow herself to get too **H**ungry, **A**ngry, **L**onely or **T**ired. I believe she said she had gotten the theory from someone who used AA. It really guided most of her life. She was very careful about not getting too hungry, angry or tired. But what I remember most is that she was very meticulous about loneliness. She chatted with many friends throughout the day, every single day. She even had friends in different time zones to chat with late into the night.

Ultimate Coping Playlist

Make the perfect coping playlist for you by giving this challenge a try. Refer to your completed playlist when you need to be entertained, revived,. etc.

Entertainment	A song that stays stuck in your head when you hear it.	A song you know all the words to.	Your favorite song from a movie.
Revival	A song that represents freedom	A song that you'd listen to fall asleep.	A song that makes you feel pumped up.
Strong Sensation	A song that reminds you of a good memory.	A song that reminds you of someone you care about	A song that reminds you of someone who cares about you
Diversion	A song that makes you feel safe.	A song you find inspirational.	Your go to positivity song.
Discharge	A song that matches your vibe you get when you feel anxious or worried.	A song that matches your vibe when you feel annoyed or angry.	A song that matches your vibe when you feel sad or afraid.

About Anger

Some have been told that depression is anger turned inward. It is a powerful emotion. Anger for many is a difficult emotion. Holding onto anger helps keep it alive. How do we get in tune with our anger? How do we just allow it to be, ride the wave, and let it dissolve in a healthy way?

It may be helpful to ask, "What are the fears behind my anger?" Can I confront the fears without getting angry?

Keep in mind that some find there are things to do in the moment, and then there is the long-term work that needs to be done in releasing emotions.

Here are some activities that may help you get through anger in the moment it appears:

- Take deep breaths
- Count to ten
- Get a change of scenery
- Talk yourself through the problem
- Throw a ball
- Keep an anger journal
- Talk about your emotions
- Exercise
- Talk with the person you are upset with after you have cooled down
- Ride a bike
- Use "I" statements when talking a problem over with someone
- Go for a walk
- Dance
- Find a safe place to scream at the top of your lungs
- Journal about your anger
- Create a letting go ritual
- Hit a pillow
- Run
- Be with the pain you feel and let it go, facing your obstacles in a positive way.
- Work with an EFT or EMDR practitioner (do not attempt on your own)

Your life is important.

When it comes to feeling suicidal, every single action that can help a person move away from the edge, no matter how small it may seem, can make a positive difference. These actions have helped many of us successfully work through a crisis.

This Safety Contract can be used to help keep you safe when you are wanting to hurt yourself. We have used this contract with many people. Making a solid promise to not hurt yourself can be powerful when the pain is so strong. If you have someone to share the Safety Contract with, have them sign the form under your signature as a witness if you'd like.

Please make as many copies as you want.

Safety Contract
a promise between me and me

I promise myself that I will not attempt to harm or kill myself in the next _____ day(s). I promise to not participate in any activity that could result in myself intentionally causing harm or death. If I am ever having thoughts of suicide, am feeling like I want to kill myself, and/or have the urge to harm myself, I will:

Remind myself that I really do care deeply for myself and do not want to harm myself.

Remind myself that I contracted not to commit suicide or harm myself.

I will call the following phone numbers, if I am feeling suicidal, but do not feel that I will harm myself immediately. (People and numbers listed can be friends, family, mental health professionals, or crisis lines).

Name   Phone Number

_____   _____

_____   _____

_____   _____

_____   _____

If I am feeling like I want to die, and or commit suicide and cannot reach the above persons, I will call 1-800-SUICIDE or 911, and ask for a CIT Officer or someone trained in mental health.

Signed_____   Date_____

Ask for help

Use this list to help you determine what to ask for from people in your life

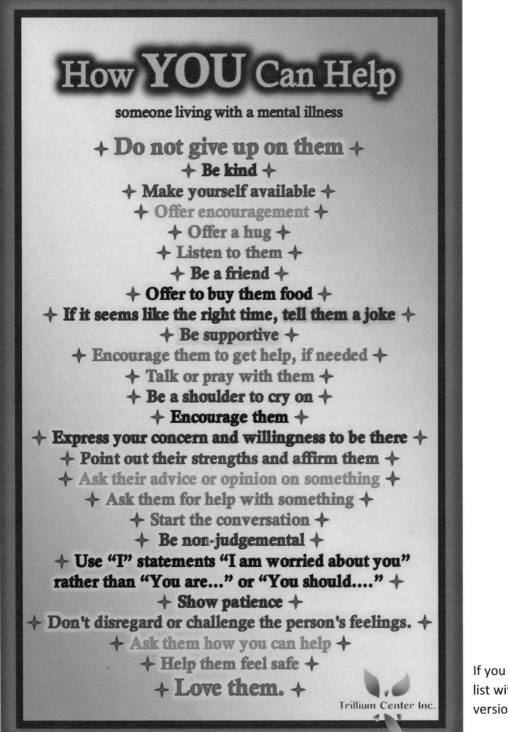

If you would like to share this list with someone, a printable version is available at:

https://TrilliumCenterInc.org/HopeAwakened.php

Introspection

The Secret about
<u>Thoughts and Feelings</u>

During my darkest days I (Cynthia) was talking with a friend and he said, "Sometimes you just have to choose to be happy."

In that moment and for years afterward I was very angry and knew he simply did not know what he was talking about. My depression just hurt. I was overwhelmed with old memories. Words stuck in my head about who others believed me to be but I simply was not that person. I just couldn't do anything. I was stuck in a miserable cycle and could not find my way out.

It's been more than 25 years since I heard the words "Sometimes you just have to choose to be happy." And I can now say I understand. And believe them. And live them.

What I know from hindsight is that thoughts and feelings are temporary and quite manageable. If I am thinking about something that is not what I *want* to think about, I can choose a different thought. If I have a feeling I don't want to feel I can choose differently there, too. The beautiful part is that it does not matter where that thought or feeling originated. Even if it is something old that a loved one said to you about you.

It took a whole lot of years for me to get to this point. But it didn't have to take so long. And I think an awful lot of people understand what I consider to be an amazing secret:

feelings change from moment to moment – more like flowing water than a concrete block.

Thoughts and feelings pass. We are in charge of what we think about and what we choose to feel. We are bigger than our thoughts and feelings. You can let both float by you like the clouds in the sky.

That is not to say all thoughts and feelings do not need to be worked on. But I can and do choose to do the work later, if needed. Lots of things helped me learn the secret. Meditation helped. Music helped. Self-help tapes helped. Reading books helped. Friends helped, even the one that made me so angry.

I realized I had reached total success with controlling my thoughts and feelings when I had to go into a meeting to negotiate a very essential contract. I had never done anything so important that could help so many people. I went into that meeting prepared by research and support. And even though I totally felt out of my league I knew I had to be successful.

I sort of put my unwanted thoughts and feelings on a shelf and went into that meeting, with what felt like false confidence. And made all of my points and convinced all who were in that meeting that I knew what I was talking about and had the documents to prove my points, too.

Later I realized the confidence was real. And I realized I had actualized the 'secret'. Now it's automatic. I don't have to choose anymore. I have internalized the process and it takes care of itself. Thoughts and feelings really are a choice and we can choose a new one any time we want. It does take work. But it's possible. I promise.

Looking at Your Current Interests

One piece of mental health recovery for some people includes creating a more full life. One that keeps a person out of their head and into activities they enjoy. Below is a table which includes many activities. Please check the appropriate column for each activity. If there are two choices, circle the one that fits you. This list was created to help inspire you to focus on what you might enjoy. There is no judgement. Extra space is provided for you to add your own activities.

Sports / Exercise	Currently Enjoy	Enjoyed in the past	Interested to learn	No interest
Baseball or Basketball				
Billiards or Bowling				
Coaching Sports				
Dancing				
Working Out				
Football or Soccer				

Outdoors / Nature / Animals	Currently Enjoy	Enjoyed in the past	Interested to learn	No interest
Bee keeping or Bird Watching				
Camping or Fishing				
Fish Tanks				
Gardening or Yardwork				
Pets or Livestock				
Running or Walking				
Stargazing				
Swimming				

Entertainment & Games	Currently Enjoy	Enjoyed in the past	Interested to learn	No interest
Attending Performances				
Board Games or Puzzles				
Checkers or Chess				
Computer Games				
Playing Cards				
Television, Movies or YouTube				

Arts / Crafts / Hobbies	Currently Enjoy	Enjoyed in the past	Interested to do	No interest
Ceramics, Pottery or Clay				
Collecting Positive Quotes				
Cooking or Baking				
Create Collages or Scrapbooking				
Drawing or Painting				
Jewelry Making or Tatting				
Molding Clay				
Needle Work				
Photography				
Reading				
Remote Control Cars				

Miscellaneous	Currently Enjoy	Enjoyed in the past	Interested to learn	No interest
Driving				
Hairstyling				
Home Decorating or Organizing				
Home or car repairs				
House Cleaning or Laundry				
Singing or Playing Instrument				
Traveling				
Writing, Blogging or Journaling				

From the above lists, pick some of your favorite interests that you have not done recently

_____   _____

_____   _____

_____   _____

_____   _____

Imagine yourself involved in any of these activities. Write how you would feel.

_____

_____

_____

What might get in the way & how could you overcome these roadblocks?

_____

_____

_____

_____

_____

Where can you pursue these interests?

_____   _____

_____   _____

_____   _____

_____   _____

_____   _____

If you need to, how can you learn more about these activities (e.g. internet, library, someone you know)?

_____   _____

_____   _____

_____   _____

_____   _____

_____   _____

Relationships

Relationships can be an influence on our wellbeing and state of mind. If our relationships are supportive and healthy, we often fare better and can thrive. If our relationships are a cause of stress, we may not fare as well.

Of course, relationships are a two way street where each party can take responsibility for their part. While there is no such thing as the perfect relationship without challenges, we can be mindful of our contributions to the welfare of the relationship. We also can learn to establish healthy boundaries, to ensure acceptable treatment by others.

Take some time to write about your current relationships.

1. Who lives in your household? _____

2. Describe your relationship(s) with them.

   _____

   _____

   _____

3. Describe relationships with family members.

   _____

   _____

   _____

4. Describe relationships with friends.

   _____

   _____

   _____

5. What about each of these relationships are supportive, joyful, healthy, and rewarding?

   _____

   _____

   _____

6. Are there improvements in your relationships that could be made?

    _____

    _____

    _____

7. How are conflicts/difficulties resolved in each of these relationships? Or not resolved?

    _____

    _____

    _____

8. What are some ways to help/support health and growth in each of these relationships?

    _____

    _____

    _____

9. What boundaries are important to you within your relationships?

    _____

    _____

    _____

10. Are you compassionate and honoring of others' boundaries?

    _____

    _____

    _____

11. How can you more effectively communicate your needs in your relationships (i.e: time, honesty, patience, etc.)?

    _____

    _____

    _____

12. If you want to, how could you meet new people?

_____

_____

_____

Robert's Story

When asked how I've reached this point of recovery my first answer is that I don't know. I can say that I fought with every fiber of my mind and body at just the simple thought that I had a mental illness. After four hospital visits, five if you include a seven day stay in detox, I gave in and had to accept what others had tried so hard to get me to see. I blame no one for my illness not even myself for the simple reason there is no blame to go around I was born this way. I can say that reaching this point wasn't easy. It took a lot of love and caring from people around me that never gave up on me and me reaching a point to where I had no other choice but to accept me for me, and the strength that my parents instilled in me to strive for more. SO I would like to share a little of me and hope that it helps and or inspires others.

Prior to my second to last hospital stay I was homeless for about a week. I began to fall into a deep depression and felt my life was over. I still had insurance from the place where I was employed and as I thought what I knew as illogical seemed very logical. In my mind I was convinced that everyone I knew and cared about would be better off if I were no longer here. I devised a plan and it was well thought out. I knew that I had $50,000 in life insurance to be divided between my two sons and wife that would double if I died an accidental death. I chose the perfect path to walk, and found the perfect place to be hit by a car going about 50 mph. So the night before I was going to put my plan into action, I called my loved ones making sure to sound calm and somewhat upbeat and without them knowing I was actually saying goodbye. I was able to speak to everyone except my oldest because he was at soccer practice; little did I know this would save my life. The next morning I started to put my plan into action. As I walked up the side street I started to go through a mental check list to make sure I hadn't left anyone out the night before. As I got close to the main street it came to me that I didn't get to say goodbye to my oldest son. I began to cry while I walked and my chest began to physically hurt. The closer I got to the main street the more my chest hurt and the harder my tears flowed. It was at this point I decided that I wasn't leaving this earth without saying goodbye to him. I saw men doing yard work so I approached them and asked them to call 911 because I was having chest pains. As the EMT's worked on me I singled one out and asked her for help because I was going to kill myself but changed my mind. I spent at least 9 hours in the emergency room until an available bed was open at a mental hospital.

I spent 7 days in that hospital and while there after some test and doctor's visits I was formally diagnosed with Bi-Polar disorder. One I refused to accept it and two against doctor's orders I fought to be released. I refused to miss my wife's birthday. Upon my release I learned that I was not welcome at my job anymore which hurt emotionally so I blocked it out. I stopped at the store and with the little money I had left I went to her house and gave her roses and wished her a Happy Birthday. Still homeless and now jobless I again ignored the prescribed medication, stopped going to the therapist and began to self medicate with drugs and alcohol. After about a week my father passed away. At this point I again went into a depression but this time was different. This time I couldn't feel anything. There was no pain, no hurt, not caring at all. After the funeral and burial I attempted to put myself back together. Though it took a while but I was able to get a job and quickly moved up to assistant manager. I had lost my car but had found a room to rent. I would have thoughts wishing that my wife would be proud of me but then reality would set in so more self medication. I also would think about my mother and father no longer with me so again more self medication. I then lost the room I was renting so again I was homeless. I found another room but I had to wait until payday to get it. The night before I was to move I was jumped and robbed. I decided at this point I was done trying and my decision to end my life was final. Again the man above stepped in and as I rode the bus the next day I happen to express to a young man that I was just tired. Somehow he picked up on what I meant and stayed with me the entire day. That evening we went to church and had a meal and then he took me to the winter shelter. Two ladies from a division of human services came by and asked to speak with me. I clearly remember one of them asking if I was thinking of harming myself and I replied, if I could find a way that was painless.

The next morning I left the shelter before the young man from the day before could attach himself to me and began my mission. I had great credit with a local drug dealer and it hit me that an overdose would do the job and not hurt, so that what I attempted to do. After an unrealistic amount of dope and beer it didn't work. It then dawned on me that maybe it just wasn't my time. I found a phone and called that division of human services to tell them that I had changed my mind. I guess that the thought that seemed clear in my head didn't translate well coming out of my mouth because they sent the police to come get me. So now again I'm at the emergency room. When I told the officer how much of the drug I had done along with how much beer I had drank he told me that I was lying because would those amounts would have killed me and I said that was the point. When the doctor came in and told me in front of the officer that I must have an angel on my shoulder and I was lucky to be alive I turned to the officer and said with sarcasm "told ya". I didn't know it then but this was the beginning of a 13 day hospital visit that would change my life.

I didn't know it then but this was the beginning of my life.

I had nothing and no place to go but I knew I had to figure out something, mainly where to sleep and how to eat. The first couple of nights I was scared but determined not to give up. I still had memories of being jumped and robbed while sleeping outside so the first thoughts where directed at finding a safe place to sleep. I don't recommend trespassing but my thought was that churches were holy ground and I would be safe there, so I found a church in a subdivision that had benches and slept there for the first few nights making sure that I was up and gone as soon as I heard the first bird chirp in the morning. After that I found an abandoned house with an aluminum shed in back and that became my home for the next two weeks. It was about the third week when the new found determination I had gained in the hospital was starting to wind down that I remembered about a place called Trillium Center. One of the groups that I had gone to while in the hospital had told me that it was a great place for people with mental health issues to go and not have to face the stigma of others.

Without knowing it I was about to open a door to the real me and join a group of people that would become my family. As I walk in for the first time I myself, without knowing was a large part of projecting the stigma on myself. I found a corner in the game room and sat there every day from open to close somewhat lost, but mostly confused. I was having a hard time accepting my disability and to be honest at first it was pissing me off that these people were walking around laughing and smiling and I couldn't, but the more I came the more I wanted to be able to feel like they did.
So every day I continued to come back and sit in my corner and everyday both staff and consumers would say hello with a smile but never pushing me to say anymore than I wanted to. Over time as I opened up more and more the Director found out I was homeless and introduced me to a young man that showed me a safe campsite. Throughout the next 18 months that's where I lived, developed friendships and began to reach a point of acceptance of not only who I was but of my situation. I also stopped attempting to assign blame. I got a job and started to look forward and started thinking of what I could do instead of what I couldn't. I would also like to think that I became a better person

because now I no longer looked at others in a judgmental or downward way because of what I had been through and seen.

I am now proud of who I am. I am a United States Veteran, a Father of two boys, a public speaker, a Certified Peer Recovery Specialist at Trillium Center and I would like to think an all around good person that enjoys helping others. I have and I say again HAVE Bi-Polar Disorder I do not suffer from this disorder. Along the way I have been able to help some and received help from many others including organizations, individuals and even my congressman.

This is just a snippet of my story and hopefully by sharing it others will benefit from it. I would like to end it this way; this is only the beginning keep your eyes and ears open for me in the future because my story has only begun.

To Be Continued !!!!!!!!!!
Robert E. Johnson III

Write a story about your life (short autobiography):

_____

_____

_____

_____

_____

_____

_____

_____

_____

_____

_____

_____

_____

_____

_____

_____

_____

_____

_____

_____

_____

_____

_____

_____

_____

_____

_____

_____

_____

_____

_____

Skill Building

Emotion and Feeling Management

Early on in her recovery process, Cynthia remembers not being able to identify her feelings. She clearly remembers, in her late 20's, receiving a sheet of paper that had about 20 feelings with faces to match and was in awe of receiving the information. Living in terror as a child left her unable to identify, process, and even feel most feelings. It took a lot of work to figure it out. That paper with all those faces and emotions still warms her heart when she thinks of it. And that feeling is joyous.

The way that German controls emotions is very personal to him. He is Christian so he actually prays about his emotions because he feels like emotions are very powerful. Emotions can change our lives and sweep us away. After prayer, German does some things. One, he talks to someone who he trusts. It can be a close friend, it can be a parent, it can be a boss. He talks with these people about his emotions because talking, to him, is a way of working them out. Also, he is receiving constructive feedback that can help him address his emotions. Those are his primary methods for taking care of his emotional state.

When Sharon leaves her aging parents' home after addressing major senior moment issues, she is quite stressed, as you may imagine. She is certain if she didn't work out the emotions, she would unfairly take it out on her elder parents or other loved ones.

Back in the day, Robert realized that if he kept his emotions in, he would get a headache. Then the feelings would store up and all of a sudden he would burst into anger at a store clerk when something wasn't quite right. Totally overreacting to the situation but he had pent up anger and it needed a target. For Robert, any unsuspecting undeserving target would do.

Cynthia had a lot of old rage because of old traumas. She didn't like feeling what she always felt and knew a change was needed. For her, it took years to work it out and find healthier ways to manage her feelings. Meditation helped. Driving helped. Doing physical labor helped. She worked hard to find a little spark of inner peace deep inside. She practiced over and over and over to bring herself back to that feeling of peace. And hold the inner peace for longer periods of time. With a whole lot of work it got easier. Now she's quite successful at managing feelings as they arise and can (most of the time) even hold an emotion and not advertise what she is feeling to those around her.

After years of trying to figure it out, some of us know what is most important, and what works, for us when managing our emotions and feelings.

This is some of what has worked for us in managing our feelings and emotions:

Acknowledge the feeling
Validate yourself
It is ok to feel what you are feeling
Be very careful about storing emotions, do your best to let them go
Act on feelings appropriately
Be honest with yourself
Be aware that feelings are not always accurate
Sometimes feelings are old from the past, looking for a current day target

We have found the following things to be helpful to us. We hope that some may be helpful for you.

Cry
Yell into a pillow, in a car, or anywhere private
Take a long hot bath
Curse
Call a friend
Whine to a friend
See a therapist
Listen to music that matches the emotion
Go for a long walk. Go for a long walk again
Breathe
Unplug for an hour. For a day. For a week.
Whine to a friend
Yell unpleasant things. Preferably in private.
Tell yourself a joke to break the stress of a moment
Write
Ride it out and know tomorrow it will be ok
Manage stress effectively

I began thinking that for some reason my mother did not love me. I felt something was wrong with me that made her not love me. I talked it over with my dad, who suggested I call a friend. The call worked.

Surprisingly, my friend admitted that he felt the same way about his mother. And other friends of his felt the same way, too.

I began to understand, through the conversation with my friend, that my perception was common among people my own age.

After further reflection, I finally realized that my mother DOES love me. Completely.

It was my perception that needed to be adjusted. I am grateful to my father and my friend for helping me figure it out. - German

Ask Myself	How often do I experience this emotion?					How do I manage this emotion?			What can I do to help manage this emotion?
"Do I feel _____"	always	frequently	sometimes	rarely	never	very well	pretty well	could do better	Some examples include write, yell, breathe, cry, call a friend, go for a walk, see a therapist, cuss, use humor, unplug for as long as necessary, listen to music that matches the emotion, etc.
alert									
acceptance									
afraid									
agitation									
angry									
annoyance									
anticipation									
anxiety									
apprehension									
attentive									
boredom									
calm									
caring									
composed									
concerned									
confident									
confused									

Ask Myself	How often do I experience this emotion?					How do I manage this emotion?			What can I do to help manage this emotion?
"Do I feel _____"	always	frequently	sometimes	rarely	never	very well	pretty well	could do better	Some examples include write, yell, breathe, cry, call a friend, go for a walk, see a therapist, cuss, use humor, unplug for as long as necessary, listen to music that matches the emotion, etc.
contentment									
curious									
defeated									
delighted									
dependence									
depressed									
despair									
dissatisfied									
distraction									
distress									
eager									
embarrassed									
emotional									
enjoyment									
excited									
exhausted									
frustration									

Ask Myself	How often do I experience this emotion?					How do I manage this emotion?			What can I do to help manage this emotion?
"Do I feel _____"	always	frequently	sometimes	rarely	never	very well	pretty well	could do better	Some examples include write, yell, breathe, cry, call a friend, go for a walk, see a therapist, cuss, use humor, unplug for as long as necessary, listen to music that matches the emotion, etc.
grouchy									
guilt									
happy									
hopeful									
hopeless									
humiliation									
hurt									
insecurity									
interested									
irritation									
isolation									
joy									
lonely									
love									
miserable									
neediness									
nervous									

Ask Myself	How often do I experience this emotion?					How do I manage this emotion?			What can I do to help manage this emotion?
"Do I feel _____ "	always	frequently	sometimes	rarely	never	very well	pretty well	could do better	Some examples include write, yell, breathe, cry, call a friend, go for a walk, see a therapist, cuss, use humor, unplug for as long as necessary, listen to music that matches the emotion, etc.
optimism									
pain									
panic									
peaceful									
pity									
proud									
rage									
sad									
satisfaction									
scared									
self-assured									
shame									
stressed									
terror									
trust									
uncomfortable									
unhappy									

Ask Myself	How often do I experience this emotion?					How do I manage this emotion?			What can I do to help manage this emotion?
"Do I feel _____"	Always	Frequently	Sometimes	Rarely	Never	Very well	Pretty well	Could do better	Some examples include write, yell, breathe, cry, call a friend, go for a walk, see a therapist, cuss, use humor, unplug for as long as necessary, listen to music that matches the emotion, etc.
upset									
vigilance									
weary									
worried									

No feeling is permanent

Mood & Activity Tracker

week of _____

Please print copies as you need them.

How was I feeling?

date →	Mon	Tues	Wed	Thurs	Fri	Sat	Sun
Happy	◯	◯	◯	◯	◯	◯	◯
Good	◯	◯	◯	◯	◯	◯	◯
Peaceful	◯	◯	◯	◯	◯	◯	◯
Grateful	◯	◯	◯	◯	◯	◯	◯
Overwhelmed	◯	◯	◯	◯	◯	◯	◯
Amused	◯	◯	◯	◯	◯	◯	◯
Irritable	◯	◯	◯	◯	◯	◯	◯
Confused	◯	◯	◯	◯	◯	◯	◯
Healthy	◯	◯	◯	◯	◯	◯	◯
Relieved	◯	◯	◯	◯	◯	◯	◯
Depressed	◯	◯	◯	◯	◯	◯	◯
Stressed	◯	◯	◯	◯	◯	◯	◯
Anxiety	◯	◯	◯	◯	◯	◯	◯
Sick	◯	◯	◯	◯	◯	◯	◯
Joyful	◯	◯	◯	◯	◯	◯	◯
Accomplished	◯	◯	◯	◯	◯	◯	◯

Daily Activities?

	Mon	Tues	Wed	Thurs	Fri	Sat	Sun
Eating	◯	◯	◯	◯	◯	◯	◯
Communication	◯	◯	◯	◯	◯	◯	◯
Concentration	◯	◯	◯	◯	◯	◯	◯
Isolating	◯	◯	◯	◯	◯	◯	◯
Sensory overload	◯	◯	◯	◯	◯	◯	◯
Sleep	◯	◯	◯	◯	◯	◯	◯
Social	◯	◯	◯	◯	◯	◯	◯
Napped	◯	◯	◯	◯	◯	◯	◯
Financial	◯	◯	◯	◯	◯	◯	◯
Hygiene	◯	◯	◯	◯	◯	◯	◯
Exercise	◯	◯	◯	◯	◯	◯	◯
Chores	◯	◯	◯	◯	◯	◯	◯

How was my day overall?

	Mon	Tues	Wed	Thurs	Fri	Sat	Sun
Good Day	◯	◯	◯	◯	◯	◯	◯
Average Day	◯	◯	◯	◯	◯	◯	◯
Bad Day	◯	◯	◯	◯	◯	◯	◯

Trillium Center Inc.

● Fill in the circle for good or positive
⊗ X through circle for not so good

About Resilience

Resilience is defined as the capacity to recover quickly from difficulties. Easier said than done, I know. What we know about resilience is that it will help with mental health struggles that stem from anything at all.

The great news is resilience is like a muscle. You can build it and strengthen it and use it to lift yourself up to feel better and create real change in your life.

Anyone can improve their resilience skills. We may have started our lives with more or less resilience than others. Our circumstances may have contributed in positive and negative ways. Wherever you are, there isn't a better time than right now to work on these skills.

Turning a plan or dream into reality entails the major aspects of building resilience: Seeking opportunities for connection, opportunities for self-reflection, opportunities for self-efficacy and mastery, and opportunities for service. Through these activities one finds social engagement, meaning, self-awareness and focus.

When we believe in the future we want, we make decisions that propel us towards that future. When it feels like life hands us opportunities, they may have been there all along. We are finally seeing them as opportunities.

You can gain resilience by being mindful of not allowing negative thoughts to gain momentum. By consciously putting your attention and focus on something even slightly more positive, you can instead build momentum in that direction. This is one tool that aids in the process of gaining resilience.

There are several factors that contribute to self-efficacy, the belief in your capability to exercise control over your own functioning and over events that affect your life. Listen to the people who encourage you. Do things you enjoy and strive to get better at them. Give yourself gentle reminders that you are worthy, and what you say and do matters.

You don't have to be a physicist. Maybe you bake awesome cookies that you share with friends and family. Maybe you follow a particular sport and love to share your knowledge and enthusiasm. Whatever gives your life meaning, go out and do it!

A wise friend told me, when I was in a very dark period, that I have a beautiful life waiting for me. She said that I might not be able to see it now because it is around a corner. I started imagining what was around that corner, and put enough attention and focus into my dream, that I began to believe it. This is not to say I don't have difficult days, but I now have plans and dreams that pull me through those days. Often I can say that I'm living the dream. *~ Sharon*

After an especially long hospital stay, my Mom helped set up volunteer opportunities for me to have structure, social opportunities and more connectedness to others. It was really helpful. I felt that I was doing meaningful work and helping others. It was a great way to bounce back (be resilient) from all I had been through. *~ Michelle*

I feel each day enables me to move closer to positive goals I have set for myself. However long it takes or which obstacles I need to work through, I can measure my success in writing them down each day. *- Kevin*

12 Tips to STRENGTHEN your RESILIENCE

Trillium Center Inc.

1. Accept YOU!
Acknowledge and accept all aspects of yourself as they are. Avoid saying "I must" or "I should." Practice self-compassion.

2. Manage Emotions
Learn to identify and be aware of your feelings. Know you do not need to take action on every feeling. Learn to take control. Use self-talk to help make an emotional shift.

3. Be Realistic
Bad things happen. We all struggle sometimes. Remind yourself that it's temporary. Whatever occurs, maintain your inner peace.

4. Believe in You
Trust your decisions. Be confident. Trust YOU. Remember what you're good at that helped you get through a tough time.

5. Be Flexible
Accept change. Find meaning in it. Practice seeing things from a different perspective. Learn and use new skills.

6. Gratitude
Focus on what you have. Don't ruminate about losses. Keep a journal. List what you appreciate, even on tough days.

7. Be Responsible
Take charge of your life, including your development. Stretch yourself outside your comfort zone. Practice setting and achieving goals. Take action.

8. Be Authentic
Reflect on, and form your unique identity. Base it on what you believe, feel, want and need. Be ok with feeling vulnerable. Express your true self.

9. Live with Purpose
Engage yourself in something you enjoy. Use your strengths to overcome challenges. See from a broader perspective. Serve others.

10. Connect
Create a network of support including role models and cheerleaders. Strengthen relationships. Reach out to share feelings and needs. Ask for help.

11. Stay Positive
Focus on your outlook and attitude. List things you're hopeful about. Use humor. Choose to be happy.

12. Practice Self-Care
Eat healthy foods. Get good rest. Exercise, even just a short walk. Get your worries out of your head with a friend or onto paper. Learn to manage your energy.

A Little About Boundaries

Boundaries, in this context, are about our personal physical space and acceptable behavior by others towards you. Some people learn healthy boundaries as they grow up. So many of us did not have that guidance and had to figure boundaries out later in life. The great news is boundaries can be learned. The diagram below illustrates general guidelines or levels of closeness & intimacy. Of course, it is different for each person. For instance, not all people place their family in the inner circle.

Boundaries can include what conversations & levels of sharing you have with others. Boundaries determine what you talk about with WHOM.

Boundaries also establish what values you have regarding behaviors you will accept from another. You might be more flexible with certain people. For example, you would probably have a wider physical boundary with acquaintances than with friends, which means the personal space around you may be more distant with acquaintances.

Remember, it is your responsibility to establish and protect your healthy boundaries. You do this, in part, by being specific, using "I" statements, being serious, firm & consistent.

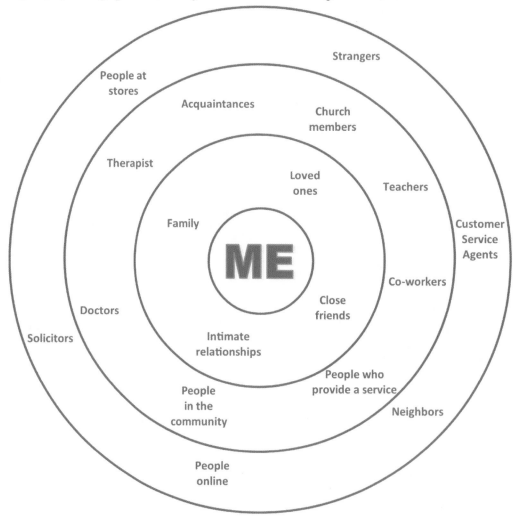

Why Boundaries are So Important

Take care of your own needs
Protect your physical and emotional space
Teach people how to treat you
Increase feelings of safety
Help protect yourself
Increase your self-esteem
Lessen your anxiety and stress
Create healthier relationships

Sample Verbal Boundary Statements
- I can stay for half an hour.
- This is something I do not want to talk about.
- I do not allow people to treat me that way.
- That is not something I want to share with you.
- No. (It's a complete sentence)
- I have done what I am willing and able to do for you. I cannot do more.
- I do not appreciate being treated that way. Stop.
- Next time you yell I will leave the room.
- You are too close. Move back.
- This is not a good time to talk (or meet, walk, etc.). Can we schedule another time for that?
- I respect your opinion but this is my life and my decision.

When someone stands too close to me at work I sometimes feel uncomfortable. So I stretch my arms out and move my arms and hands around at about a foot or two away from my body and try to say with humor:

"You are in my bubble!"

People that I have used this tactic with have always given me space, and it seems they remember it in the future, too. ~ Cynthia

Non-Verbal Boundary Setting
- Sometimes not responding is a clear boundary-setter
- If someone is standing too close, step backward.
- Break eye contact with a person and don't reconnect
- Fold your arms across your chest
- Don't verbally engage
- Shake your head silently in disagreement
- Walk away

Actions Some May Never Tolerate
- Being yelled at
- Being called a name
- Being sworn at
- Uncomfortable physical distance
- Someone oversharing personal information
- Invasion of privacy-personal files, email, etc.
- Time monopolizing
- Lying
- Being gossiped about
- Sharing my personal info with others
- Manipulation

Here is a boundary circle that you can fill out for yourself. List people in your life and think about how close you would like to be with them and place them in the appropriate circle. Remember this is for you, based on how you feel. There is no judgement or comparison, just a way to help understand your own personal boundaries.

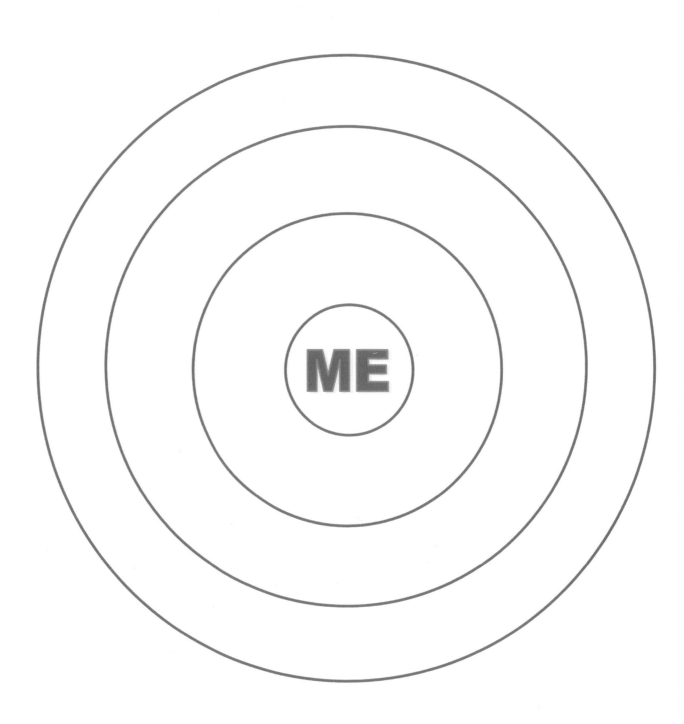

What boundary issues are currently challenging you and how can you address them?

Who	Issue	Possible Solution
SAMPLE Roommate	Talks too much	Set a time limit for conversation
_____	_____	_____
	_____	_____
_____	_____	_____
	_____	_____
_____	_____	_____
	_____	_____
_____	_____	_____
	_____	_____

Let's Talk About Affirmations

I am sometimes mean to myself. My name is Michelle. When I looked over some of the lists we have included in this book, I felt an internal push for all the good things. How good, wonderful & fun it would be to actually do them. Then my inner voice crept up and said some mean things. Immediately I recognized I often look for external permission to allow myself to be kind to ME. There just simply seems to be a negative voice within that prevents me from creating the life I know I deserve.

When I recognize this negative inner voice, I have the ability to instead choose a positive statement or affirmation to turn the tide to positivity. "I choose to be happy," is a truthful choice that I make to fight all those mean and unhelpful thoughts.

The best affirmations are the ones you come up with yourself. I want to share with you my passion for affirmations. It is possible to thoughtfully choose what your mind focuses on and to choose words that will help your mental health, rather than harm it.

Affirmations could be boiled down to: words you say to yourself. So that means there is such a thing as negative affirmations, but some of us choose to focus on positive affirmations. It's like your mind is the soil, and depending on the affirmation seeds that you sow, is what will be produced in your life. Also, like gardening, it takes some care and patience for good things to grow. You have to make a concerted effort to focus on the positive thoughts [affirmations] you have set out for yourself.

The word habit is an important one concerning affirmations. Saying an affirmation once will not do you nearly as well as saying it over and over; in other words, habitually. Positive, to the point, words said over and over either out loud and/or inside your mind can be quite powerful. You have this choice.

I believe that all people struggle with negativity at one time or another. Many times, we don't even realize it. However, if you catch yourself wallowing in negative thoughts, you can use a "jolt" of positivity (an affirmation) to get back to a better place. But it's the everyday repetition of your affirmations that will do you the most good. I hope you learn to "wallow in happy thoughts" while creating your own helpful affirmations.

On the following page are affirmations that some of us have found helpful. Please use them if you so choose or create some specifically for yourself.

- I am a good person
- I do the best I can
- I can make this day better
- I've got this
- I am amazing
- My hard work pays off
- I really will be alright
- I am alright
- I love myself
- Good things are coming
- The positive voice wins.
- I take control of me. Watch out world as I do so!
- I love my job
- I allow myself to be kind to ME
- I make the step to do something fun
- It is ok for me to do fun things
- It is important that I make time to do fun things
- I need 'fun thing time' in my life
- I choose positivity especially when I sense the negative voice
- It is so important to choose positivity – it can be a matter of life and death
- Fun is wonderful
- I can love myself
- I like myself

Two things to remember about affirmations: They work best written in the present tense, like they've already happened. Second, repetition is key. Say your favorite affirmation over and over, out loud and in your mind. Use stickies around the house or on your mirror or somewhere you see when you wake up.

Affirmations can and should be modified to resonate for you. We've noticed that sometimes a person is not quite ready for positive affirmations. That is okay and you can create wording appropriate for where you are. Sometimes to have an affirmation feel right, start with something like "I'm open to the possibility of…" "I am open to the possibility that good things are coming" "I can allow myself to be kind to ME."

You can use these affirmations, modify them for yourself and/or add some of your own:

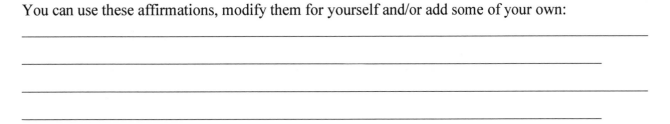

A Turn Toward the POSITIVE

What is a good childhood memory for me?

_____

_____

Now that I know what I know, what might I have chosen differently in my life?

_____

_____

What have I done that makes me feel proud?

_____

_____

What activities make me lose track of time in a peaceful, positive way?

_____

_____

What talents do others see in me?

_____

_____

What would others say they like best about me?

_____

_____

What animals do I like?

_____

_____

If I could travel anywhere, where would I go and why?

If I could only keep five possessions, what would they be?

_____

_____

_____

_____

_____

YOU ARE YOU,
AND THAT IS YOUR
ADVANTAGE.

What last made me cheer?

_____

_____

What teacher made a positive impact on me, how and why?

_____

_____

What was a positive defining moment in my life?

_____

_____

What am I grateful for in this moment?

_____

_____

What is my favorite season? Why? What do I like to do during that season?

_____

_____

Who do I admire and why?

_____

_____

What are some of my favorite books and why?

_____

_____

How does love feel to me?

_____

_____

How does joy feel to me?

_____

_____

What have I done that has brought joy to others?

_____

_____

What are my strongest qualities?

_____

_____

What is a skill I'd like to learn and why?

_____

_____

What does a perfect day look like to me?

_____

_____

What does a perfect job look like to me?

_____

_____

If I could have a positive impact in my community or on the world, in what way would I?

_____

_____

How do I visualize my success?

_____

_____

How can I come back from a setback?

_____

_____

What are my strengths?

_____

_____

What strengths have others said they see in me?

_____

_____

How can I make a positive change in my life?

_____

_____

How can I accomplish my goals?

_____

_____

How can I be of service to others?

_____

_____

How can I encourage others to be their best?

_____

_____

Who is my mentor?

_____

_____

What compliments have I received?

_____

_____

What do I do that others have admired?

_____

_____

What makes me happy?

_____

_____

My Self Care Priorities

Activities I enjoy

People I enjoy and trust

Hygiene goals

What I do to relax

Healthy foods I like

DO'S AND DON'TS

✓ DO'S

- Do plan ahead and create a schedule

- Do give yourself at least 20 minutes for self-care

- Do reward yourself regularly to make self-care fun

✗ DON'TS

- Don't put off your self-care

- Don't rush to practice self-care

- Don't beat up on yourself if you have a tough day

Exercise & movement I enjoy

Set Your Goals

GOAL

STEPS

- [ ]
- [ ]
- [ ]
- [ ]
- [ ]
- [ ]
- [ ]
- [ ]
- [ ]
- [ ]

I NEED HELP WITH

RESOURCES

THIS GOAL IS IMPORTANT TO ME BECAUSE

Claiming My Power - Michelle

A few years ago, I went through an extremely tough time, both mentally and physically. Part of it was suffering from psychosis. That really was a time where I was focused on surviving. I forgot that people do not usually stay in mental hospitals forever. I was not in touch with the hope of knowing or even wishing that the difficult things wouldn't last forever. Most of it was such a confusing and utterly terrifying time for me.

It wasn't all that long ago that I remembered that after every psychotic event I've had in my life, it took years to really recover. I could feel myself not wanting to give this recent experience the time needed to heal. Once I realized that, I started to think, "What the heck! Why should this time be so different from the others?" I have had a hate relationship with the word acceptance/or being accepting, so it hasn't been easy. In truth, the adage 'time heals all wounds' is a big part of this personal healing of mine. The passing of time, regardless of how much effort I make or not, seems to be a great big helper in the healing.

I would be remiss if I didn't mention how much I still struggle, as evidenced by the work that my therapist and I continue to do. Only very recently, I had a real breakthrough session with my therapist. Understand that I have been going to therapy in general for years and we have been working particularly hard on getting to a better place after my difficult time a few years ago. A friend of mine helped me process some of these thoughts, as well. I recently took some notes on that breakthrough session. I thought I would share, in case it might help someone.

- I can decide if I am going to move forward when anger hits about something that happened in the past. The fact that I have choice, even concerning what I think are difficult feelings, is one of the most powerful things I learned.

"I DON'T HAVE TO CLING TO THE TRAUMAS TO FEEL SPECIAL"

- What do I do when anger or sadness comes? I am to think about: What does wallowing in these feelings do for me? Truth: It keeps me from enjoying and being in the present. It also, in fact, does me no good. Here's the big one: I get to choose what I wallow in or not. Claiming my power is amazing.
- I have to make a decision today to live in the present. Yep, every day, making that decision.
- I am special just because I am. I don't have to cling to the traumas to feel special. I was using my traumas as a way to feel special, and it was one reason I wasn't allowing myself to heal from them.
- The traumas aren't serving me well. Again, another way of stating that it is better for me to do the work and allow myself to heal.
- I already lived through it once and made it through; I don't need to live it over and over again.

I focus on peace in my heart, and I have found ways to return to that feeling if something seems to get in the way of it. Even though COVID makes life difficult, I've been able to hold on and not go down too deep of a rabbit hole into sad emotions, mostly. I am a person who takes medicine.

Keeping up with that, sometimes by setting alarms on my phone, is very important to me. I think taking it consistently is helping greatly in keeping my mood even.

When I get sad, part of it sometimes seems to be because I am physically tired. Not too long ago I heard of something called "sleep hygiene." There are actual YouTube videos on it, if you type it in there. I am just beginning to allow myself the down time to set myself up for a good night's sleep. And to put away my favorite 'blue light' devices (phone, tablet) to help the cause as well.

Believe me, I still have sad thoughts, ruminate or obsess about the past, thriving is not a place of perfection or having no problems. It's a place of being able to handle problems when they come. I feel myself being on an even keel and being able to think clearly and being in touch with the good in life. I wonder if some people take all those things for granted, but having been in places in my life where these simple things were not possible for me, I have joy because they are my present reality. I have gratitude for another day to try.

Thrive

So the definition of thrive seems a little vague.

thrive

/THrīv/

prosper; flourish.

For some, it is such a powerful word. We have collected stories of people who are thriving in life and are sharing them with you in this section of our workbook. Each person's life looks different from everyone else's, but they certainly all have some things in common. Some of those things are: understanding the power of giving back to their communities, finding balance in their lives, living a self-directed life, and living with purpose. And they all understand the power of positivity and gratitude.

Every one whose stories are included in this THRIVE section has struggled mightily. Most with suicide attempts. Some with substance use. All with intense and serious mental health issues. Now they are thriving.

Raymond eventually learned **"The Secret About Thoughts & Feelings."** It took him some time to figure it out. His life was full of some struggles and dark existence for quite a few years. Somehow, after recovery found him, Raymond realized he did not have to accept what his father had been saying to him about him. He could step out of that reality and truly begin to live. Raymond learned and now exhibits great **"Boundaries."** But he had to learn. He joined a recovery community that helped him get on the right path, his path. Now Raymond is living a beautiful life with purpose. He is a huge influence in many other people's lives.

Cynthia vividly remembers the day she had a massive panic attack at work. And Sharon, in her gentle nature, introduced Cynthia to the 4-7-8 Breathing Method which is described in the **"Exercises That May Help"** page of this workbook. Sharon guided Cynthia through the exercise a few times. And many years later, that moment is seared into Cynthia's memory and her soul. Even though, in her early years, Cynthia did not feel like she had any **"Reasons for Living,"** in hindsight she can now see that there were many reasons, but her depression simply did not allow her to acknowledge it. Cynthia has been in a great psychological place for a couple of decades. Her passion is mental health recovery, and she does everything she can to help others in her community.

Kevin is amazing at sharing positive energy. He learned the power of positivity in his own life during his mental health struggles. Kevin had fabulous input into the **"A Turn Toward the Positive"** worksheets. He is very devoted to sending out positive messages, both in person and in text messages with those he serves and the lucky people in his support system. Kevin clearly has a very strong **"Ultimate Coping Playlist"** that he had created for himself in order to have music to match his mood. The people that ride in his vehicle mention the eclectic tastes he has in music that he plays while he drives.

Sharon amazes us with her level of **"My Self-Care Priorities."** She keeps track of how she is doing throughout the day and takes care of her needs when she identifies them. She is great at clearly stating her need when she is with others. Sharon is an example for others in understanding and living **"A Little About Boundaries."** During her growing years, her parents were able to teach her a baseline for how Sharon could expect to be treated by others, her mother even coming to her defense in situations that demanded it. Later in life, Sharon recognized that she also learned about boundaries by observing other people. She understands self-awareness is key in creating and maintaining healthy boundaries. Sharon provides a beautiful example for so many other people. Sharon is definitely living her purpose and is living the dream.

Michelle has learned a whole bunch **"About Anger."** Most would not realize it because she is a joy to be around but she has carried old anger for a long time now. Mostly, it seems, it is directed toward her mental health challenges. Michelle now understands better how to process anger in a healthier manner and can even understand when it is time to simply let the anger go. One of her passions in her mental health recovery is **"Affirmations."** Michelle uses positive affirmations in her personal life to change her thoughts. She is often seen or heard encouraging others to do the same. Affirmations are powerful to her and have had a strong impact for Michelle.

Mike tells a powerful story of his life. He struggled a bunch and finally decided to awaken. Once he found hope, it inspired him to look at his **"Relationship"** with other people. He took a big step and distanced himself from the toxic people in his life that were not healthy for him. Mike took an inventory of his **"Current Interests"** and created a life that he cherished. After so many years of dark times, Mike is living and thriving and helping many other people in his journey.

Brien lived with using substances for a bunch of years. He was self-medicating with alcohol. With some help of friends, Brien created an amazing **"Foundation to Mental Health Recovery"** for himself, which he is still using today. He knows about structure, and boasts about making his bed every single day. He's created a strong network of people who he cares about and who care about him. Brien is also a master of **"Coping Skills."** He knows when to make a call to someone, to reach out and connect. He's wildly artistic and gets to create and perform music with his band. He knows the power of gratitude and clearly lives with joy in his heart.

We are grateful to all the people who have generously shared a part of their story in this section of **Hope Awakened**. They all spent many years merely surviving. They have all worked hard at learning and developing the various skills that are included in this book and other skills, too. Perhaps the biggest step they took was to commit. Commit to themselves.

After years of hard work and what often felt like psychological torture, the people sharing their stories in this section are truly living a life of their own choosing. A life they created and one they cherish. Those sharing their stories for you here are thriving. In their own very unique ways.

They are all certain you have a force within you to guide you on your path.

YOU can learn to thrive.

Champion for Mental Health Recovery - Kevin

Kevin is a champion for his own mental health recovery. He developed a system for his recovery that is working for him beautifully and he often shares it with others in his work as a Certified Peer Recovery Specialist. He sees his tools for mental health recovery as a stool with legs. The top of the stool, where one would sit, is Mental Health. Each leg represents a coping skill or area of life that he uses for his personal wellness. His Wellness Stool has four legs, which are comprised of:

> Support Network
> Physical Wellness
> Spirituality & Positivity
> Recreation

Kevin routinely, on a daily basis, checks in with himself on these four key areas in his life. His support network is his social circle, which includes all the people he can talk with about personal issues and give and receive support. The mental health professionals in his life include a psychiatrist and often a therapist.

His physical wellness is one of his top priorities. His exercise routine includes moving all day long (we rarely see him sit down) and making sure he gets a long walk 6 days a week. He also stretches, does calisthenics, resistance and sometimes yoga. For his nutrition, Kevin eats pescatarian meals and is committed to eating healthy, clean food to the extent that he is able.

Having attended a Catholic high school, religion and spirituality is a huge piece of life's puzzle for Kevin. He finds strength, peace and tranquility in his relationship with God. For him, positivity is also connected to his spirituality. He often offers words of encouragement and has a list of his support network who he texts positive, happy messages to on a regular basis to share his good vibe and provide support to them.

He is very careful about what he watches on television and listens to on the radio. He's the band KISS' number one fan. His taste in music is very eclectic and he will find the music to match his mood or emotion.

Each of the four legs of his Wellness Stool is monitored carefully. If he feels symptoms coming up, he will check in with himself in these four areas first. If he has not connected to his support network, he will reach out immediately. If he's feeling over-stressed, he will take a longer walk or have a talk with someone who he trusts.

When old pain creeps up for Kevin, he knows he needs to sit with it, let it dissipate naturally, understanding that he is bigger than what he is currently experiencing and honors himself by allowing the feelings to pass.

Kevin is admired by many people in his community. He is a fantastic peer support group facilitator and has been doing that for fourteen years. He is low key and gentle and is gifted with the special ability to talk to just about anyone. The Wellness Stool is something that he personally came up with, uses himself and has been sharing for years with others. After struggling for many years with extreme mental health challenges, he has created a formula for his Wellness Stool that keeps him on track. It allows him to live a blessed life and to thrive.

This is how Kevin's Wellness Stool looks:

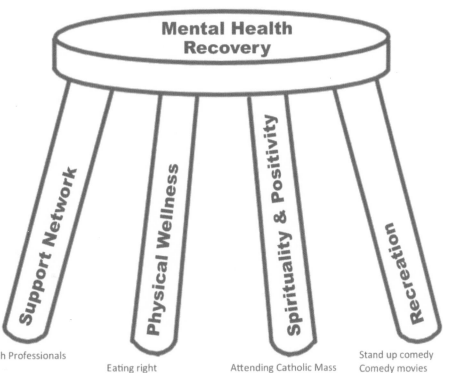

Support Network	Physical Wellness	Spirituality & Positivity	Recreation
Mental Health Professionals	Eating right	Attending Catholic Mass	Stand up comedy
Goal Setting	Lots of vegetables	Meditation	Comedy movies
Emotion Management	Exercise	Positive Goals	Music
Family	Getting enough sleep	Prayer	Rock
Close people in my support circle	Vitamins	Texting positive messages	Jazz
Mentors	Medication	Time with others	Country
Listen to and apply what I learn	Walking	Positive affirmations	Christian
Catholic Church	Stretching	Read my Bible	Classical
Journaling	Resistance	Read about other spiritual	All music, really
Auto Mechanic	Going to parks	& religious teachings	Reading about things I enjoy
guides me on repairs	Being in nature		Cars
	Having 'downtime'		Renewable energy
	Making smoothies		Financial information
			Eating at various ethnic restaurants
			Travel
			Home improvement
			House cleaning
			Telling corny jokes
			Biking at the beach
			Learn about Environmental Concerns

Now create your own

Wellness Stool!

Living the Dream - Sharon

I've had panic attacks as long as I can remember, but they were rare, and most were manageable. When my first marriage fell apart I slid, over about two months, into a 24/7 state of panic. I became less and less functional during the day, I wasn't sleeping well, and my dreams were pretty awful when I did sleep. I thought I could tough it out, that it would pass. I'd been through some rough stuff before and made it through alright. This time I was not so lucky. I tried therapy and went to a chiropractor for back and neck pain related to the stress. I got a full physical and tried medication. Some things helped and some made things worse.

I realized that healing from this was going to be a slow process. I started learning everything I could about anxiety and what feeds it. There were days when all I could do was to get through the next minute, and then the next one. I watched British comedies. I read. I ate a lot of apples, because crunching on them gave me moments of feeling okay. I cooked a lot because cooking did that for me, too. I could get lost in the process.

My path to thriving included figuring out that I have celiac disease, so I have to be on a gluten free diet. I also work hard at releasing stress through exercise, yoga, limiting caffeine, managing my responses to thoughts and being aware of my own stress responses. I have found supplements and mindfulness exercises that are good for calming my nervous system. I am not free of anxiety, but it does not control me. I look for beauty, so I find it everywhere.

These days I have a wonderful job, and I'm married to a wonderful partner. I not only dream about cruising to Europe on a sailboat, I'm taking actions to get there. I'm in a position to be available for my parents as they age and sometimes need help.

Life can be frickin' hard, but there is also so much joy, wonder, and beauty.

Just Simply Me! - Raymond

Thriving, the meaning of thriving to me is to prosper, flourish or gain in spite of or because of one's overall circumstances.

I look at my life simply as I this, am I thriving or am I simply surviving. To me there is enormous difference. I struggled in my substance use and mental health issues, in fact all throughout my early life; I had the overall feeling that I did not know where I belonged. I had that feeling that there was something that I was supposed to do but I did know what it was and I did not not know how to go about finding out. This forced, if you will, a tremendous amount of struggle in my life.

So way before any recovery that I have (15 plus years, 5712 days) I had mental health issues and struggles. I mean all I did was exist. I always would choose that path of the least resistance because it was just easier for me to go alone and not have to apply much to it. I reacted to any and all situations so that I wouldn't have to respond at all. I became good, so I thought, at blaming and complaining about any and everything. My feeling of failure was also enhanced by my father constantly telling me that "I wouldn't be anything in life."
So I started to believe him because it meant that I did not have to step up to fail, I was already failing. I remember feeling stuck, unworthy and unauthentic, although I didn't know what that meant at the time. Just plain worthless!

This was my life and I had no clue on how to get off of this daily, hourly and sometimes minutely merry-go-round of mental anguish.

Then all of a sudden, or so it seemed, I found Recovery or did it find me. Recovery from my mental health as well as recovery from the substance use addict that I had become. It started with me being willing to be willing, understanding that I did not have to give in to anyone else's plans and design or thoughts of what or who I should be. Once I got on a continuous path of recovery, all things seemed, no all things did in fact turn in a very positive direction. I was engaged in me and I was "Thriving" at it. I started to accomplish things as I began to thrive and not sabotage my next step. I became willing to be willing, I admitted to my self that I wanted to thrive and not struggle. That in itself was a huge turning point in my life.

Now I, Raymond T. Barnes am the Division Head of Peer Services for the Norfolk Community Services Board.
Now I am a Certified Peer Recovery Specialist for the State of Virginia.
Now I am a Certified Peer Trainer for the State of Virginia.
Now I am me , not what anyone else may or may not think of or about me.
Just Simply Me!
Today I Thrive!!!

Finding the Good in Life - Michelle

One of the greatest positives of my life was receiving my degree from George Mason University. This was not an easy process. My mental health issues got diagnosed while I was in high school. I experienced them again in college, partly from trying to take a Herculean amount of credits in one semester, as well as other issues. After surviving the bout with my mental illness, I volunteered and slowly re-entered the workforce for a few years which helped me go back to the university. I realized I needed to slow it down and go my own speed. Altogether, it took me a total of 13 years from start to finish. That was a joyous moment. When I look back on that, I am able to revel in the one major quality that helped me through. Perseverance.

After graduation, I was very happy to get a job at a local newspaper. When I quit after having worked there for two years, I felt like I left the place in a bad way. Now I see that I was very unkind to myself and obsessively ruminated on what I must have done wrong. I curled inward, getting to the point that I only left home for doctor's appointments or for reasons that seemed absolutely necessary. I slept until what I called 'Oprah time,' meaning 4 p.m. daily when her show came on, only getting up so that I could make dinner for my husband.

It was difficult for me to get out into the world again. Managing myself was, to put it mildly, a struggle. I stayed in my comfort zone, continuing to not leaving home very much at all. Grocery shopping meant going to just one store. My life was limited, as I lived with depression and fear that lasted for years. Thankfully, a friend invited me out into the world to a safe space. This was the beginning of a magical resurgence for me. After a few visits with my friend, I heard about a baking program which taught people marketable skills for employment.

It took two tries, but I graduated from that baking program and began to see a lift in my self-esteem and a bit of an expansion in my comfort zone. I began volunteering for a local non-profit which quickly turned into employment.

In the early few years of my employment, I started and managed a dynamic speaker's bureau for our community. It is a program for people with lived experience of mental illness who speak about their mental health recovery. Soon after, I and other co-workers joined with a social worker on an international project, which facilitated an opportunity for me to be a speaker at the United Nations in New York City.

I had physical and mental health concerns surface between 2014-17. My focus quickly shifted from creating projects and opportunities to what my employer refers to as cocooning, in order to heal.

Skip forward to now, and I was so amazed and honored, frankly, to be asked to be a person to write about thriving. Believe it or not, it has been very difficult for me to write this section. I needed help remembering, thinking and writing the good stuff. I have so much to, dare I say, celebrate and find joy in. It really is with a grateful heart that I find myself waking up and rising each day as a person in reality (as opposed to a person experiencing psychosis). I am grateful to be here and living what thrive means to me.

I am lucky that through it all, my marriage to my soulmate still endures. The two of us are definitely a team in life. Including my husband, I have created a wonderful support system of people who care deeply for me. I am recently, successfully, reconnecting with folks I went to college with. I am trusted, respected, and have become a rock for co-workers. One co-worker referred to me as the nicest person he has ever worked with. My gentle nature simply brings out the best in people.

In addition to having strong relationships, I have learned a lot about myself and life in general. I am quick to pick up new hobbies that will challenge me, but my favorites include creating jewelry or other crafty kind of items and learning about cooking healthy meals and smoothies in my Vitamix. I am learning the ukulele and I play simultaneously with a friend over Zoom. I am just starting to learn chess, too. Chess was the catalyst for when my parents met. I always joke that I wouldn't be here if it weren't for chess!

Over the years, I have learned how to be a strong advocate for myself. After missing some medications at times, I figured out how to use a medication organizer, and keep reminder alarms set on my phone so I can best stay on track. When the housing market went topsy-turvy a few years ago, even though I am not financially savvy, without hesitation I went through the complicated process of refinancing the mortgage for my family. When Instacart got up and running in our area, I knew they were the perfect solution to my physical issues of not being able to do the grocery shopping. I feel like they may be one of the best things to come out of the Covid epidemic. When carpal tunnel started giving me pains in my arms, I was direct when consulting with the doctor and she knew to suggest the right treatment to use at night. I am faithful in wearing the braces to help fix the problem without surgery.

My newest technique for my mental health wellness is to ask myself: "What is this emotion doing for me?" If the current emotion will not create a positive or constructive outcome, I know to quickly change or even block the emotion and bring my thoughts to something more positive that affects my well-being in a positive way.

I quickly admit that I am a work in progress. But I know for sure how important it is to stay in my happy place, not allowing myself to get too high or too low. I am committed to always finding the good in life.

From the bottom of my heart, I believe you can find the good in life, too.

Find the good in life

Putting the Pieces Together - Mike

I can't share every meaningful experience, but I hope that what I share will fit with a theme. I won't share with you any diagnoses that were given. I want you to remember this story has a happy ending.

From one of my journal entries years ago "Where does all the time go? I've lost so much. It runs through my fingers. I'm shaking, my body hurts. I'm ashamed. Shame, shame."

I've experienced thousands of moments like this. Some of you may have felt some things very similar very recently. Maybe even at this very moment. For decades, thoughts of taking my life have been a persistent threat...dozens of times a day.

I have gone through many very dark times. That includes self-medicating and using illicit substances, toxic relationships, terrifying fear in a large city including curling up in a ball on the sidewalk, crying in the cold rain. Living with fear so overwhelming that I wanted to scream out loud. Someone asked me, "Have you ever given up, Michael?" The answer is, "Yes, many times."

To begin my journey, I had to get real with myself with where I was at. The commitment I could finally keep with myself, living in transitional housing, was to get out of bed for 5 minutes and sit in the chair at the side of my bed. I had to get over myself, that I was a "grown man" and should be able to do more. I had to get over everyone else's expectations of what I could or should do.

I would get up for 5 minutes, then I could get back in bed if I wanted. Sometimes I did, sometimes I didn't. But, I always kept that commitment. I did that for two weeks, then increased the time to 10 minutes. Next, the commitment was to go out of my room to the front room for 10 minutes, then go back if I wanted. Then the porch. Then the corner near the house, then the park.... It went on from there. Finally, 9 years late, I went 2,800 miles away for a job across the Country.

I could not have done it without starting sitting in that chair right next to the bed 5 minutes a day. That got me to 2,800 miles.

After so many years of struggling, I finally decided to awaken. To try again. I was experiencing clarity, revelation, and hope. There were some things that began to happen when I found hope.

- I began to journal daily.
- I got rid of toxic people in my life.
- I opened books of scripture and read and read.
- I began applying for benefits.
- Started writing short stories.
- I put myself through a boot camp of sleep hygiene
- Eliminated watching screens
- Got donations to start a community garden
- Attend a 12 step recovery program
- Joined the cast of a musical
- Restarted therapy

Sometimes when the pieces come together, they just come together. Frankly, sounds like it could be too much, doesn't it? Like I'm setting myself up for failure. That's a reasonable thought. But let's hold that thought.

Many individuals and families who go through the awful experience of distressing thoughts, feelings, and behaviors look for "The Answer." Even when we're pretty sure it doesn't work, we think it really should. That there really SHOULD be "The Answer." Sometimes we think taking meds is "The Answer," or getting a job, or stop using the addictive substances or frequent services or hospitalization. There are many places we look for "The Answer." And all of these can be work on their own. And generally we need more than a few things, we need many pieces. A secret I've found is sometimes even with all the pieces not everything that ails us goes away.

Today I'm married, have two children, a wonderful job, great career, and rich life. Some pleasures – volunteerism and incredible opportunities, but also today I'm not free of my conditions. Sometimes I still experience the same things I did before. But my life is beyond my wildest dreams. Simple, clear moments are what I live for now.

I have more than I ever thought I could. It took years of walking through hell again and again. I only shared a portion with you today. Importantly, I'm not sad how my life turned out. Even with the decades of pain. I used to regret I didn't have the childhood everyone else did. RIIGHT!!! Like I *thought* everyone else did. But without the pain I wouldn't be here now. I wouldn't be the man I am today.

I love my life. I have more than I ever knew possible, but I'm not perfect.

I challenge you to find your pieces. Keep looking. If you give up for a little while, when you're ready…try some more! You can find your pieces. You can become your best self.

Recovery: An Ongrowing Experience - Brien

I am a certified Peer Recovery Specialist and I work at the Community Services Board for Fairfax County in Emergency Services. I absolutely love what I do. I'm a father, musician, poet, author, and I also recently became a grandfather. If I wasn't in recovery, none of this would be possible: the job that I have, the relationships that I've built, the opportunities that I've been given, the music that I get to be a part of, and the fact that I was able to put a book together. I really want to put that out there, that none of this would have been possible, without being in recovery. While I was actively burning my life to the ground, destroying people's trust, and my self-esteem, no one was asking me, "Hey, would you come and share your story in this book we're putting together? Because we really want to read about how you're doing that." A little snarky, but it's my truth. What has since changed is I'm engaged in a network of support, and I'm part of my community.

I love words, so I looked up the word striving. It means to devote serious effort and energy, and the word thriving means to grow vigorously, to flourish. I believe that is my story through the ups and downs, and through it all. The language I use has become very important to me - the way I refer to others, and the way I refer to myself. We are not our diagnosis. I'm not Brien 'Depression' Stewart. I have dyslexia; I have depression. I like to think of these as challenges, not destinations.

My recovery journey started with coming to the realization that I couldn't fix myself with myself. I had tried. I tried self-medicating with alcohol, and with other things. Those weren't working. I even went years without doing any kind of self-medicating, but also without being engaged in any kind of recovery or growth. I refer to those as my years of Sodriety: just dry, not truly sober. The situation I grew up in, the household I grew up in, was awful. I saw things first graders shouldn't see. I remember being four years old thinking, "Someday I won't be here." I kept pretending I was a roommate in this house I was born into. I spent many years trying to be quiet and invisible. I learned how to laugh in silence – when I was able to laugh at all. My fantasy became my reality when I was seven years old and I was removed from that environment and placed into the foster care system for several years.

One of the positive things that came out of my foster care experience was that I was introduced to therapy and learned the importance of speaking out loud in a therapeutic environment. While actively engaged in therapy, I learned what unconditional support felt like. It was something that I was part of from age nine to about thirteen. Then from thirteen to an older age I lost that skill - like if you're working out and stop doing it, you lose muscle. I lost muscle memory, began drifting, and that's when my self-medicating with alcohol and drugs began. Several years later, I ended up back in therapy.

I believe that my years of Sodriety were truly the darkest years of my life because I didn't have any coping skills. It was like roaming the earth with no skin - overreacting constantly. Everything was so painful and uncomfortable. Then I ran into two people I hadn't seen in years. They were absolutely on fire for life. I wanted what they had; I didn't know what it was, I just knew that I didn't have it or know how to achieve it. They told me, "We dove into recovery and followed the suggestions of other people in recovery. Call us when you're ready." A few weeks later, I don't know what happened, I think the pain got great enough, I was given a gift of desperation coupled with impending doom. I called them. They brought me to a twelve-step recovery meeting where I felt safe for the first time in a long time. The first guy I met was so helpful. He gave me the greatest truth I've ever heard. He said, "I'm not going to promise you that your life is going to get better because you're involved in recovery, but I will promise you that your life is going to get different, because *you* are going to get different. The way you view life and think of yourself is going to get different, and by getting different, it might just get better, too."

I used to think recovery was a one and done kind of thing. I'd take a class or go to a few meetings, and maybe someone would say something that would fix everything. What I've come to understand about my recovery journey is that it's just that – a journey, and the longer I remain on it, the more I discover. I would say for me, it's not about doing a bunch of things a few times. My recovery journey has been about doing a few new things many, many times. I make my bed every day. I can't leave my house without making my bed. I check in with my network every day. These things were once something I felt I had to do, then I *wanted* to do them, and now I *get* to do them.

In the last couple of months, I've had a lot of extremes happen, some that were great and some that were not so pleasing. I got into a relationship and then it ended. And then I became a grandfather and

I got to meet this beautiful, new little person. And then a few weeks later my adopted mother died. And then I got to record a new record with my band. With each up and down, I remained active and engaged in my recovery. I have to remember that each day that I wake up, all of this is stuff I get to do and be part of, and I certainly want to tap into as much gratitude as possible. I believe having gratitude is like having a superpower. The longer I stay engaged and the more comfortable I become with this idea, the truer this statement is.

My book is called, *Aim to Reach: Poetry, Recovery, and Punk Rock Stories*. It spans from 1986 to 2021. I'd thought about creating it for a long time. Then I was inspired by this quote from the famous philosopher, David Lee Roth: "When is the last time you did something for the first time?" I remember thinking, "I've been wanting to do this, now's the time!" I just started outlining it and it came together very quickly. It's 35 years of my story in music, and a lot of recovery, anything I learned that I really felt changed my heart and my thoughts. It's doing well, which is an exciting surprise and a delight.

The big thing I came up with recently was this: I used to believe the darkness of all I had been through – my childhood environment, my foster care experience, my self-medication attempts - was the lock. I believed I was locked into this way of being, this way of thinking. When in fact, the darkness was not the lock. It actually turned out to be the key. It led me to the point where I had to try something different if I wanted to feel and be someone different.

Everything I have, my peace of mind, my serenity, my joy, is all from recovery. I was in so much pain for so long and I didn't even know it. If someone feels they are far from striving or thriving, I would say try to do any little positive thing. One of the biggest gifts I got out of my peer support training is to meet yourself where you are. Give yourself credit for showing up to life. Open the window shades. What are you grateful for? Try to figure out the one thing you can do to bring light.

Simply Blessed - Cynthia

I have been pondering this piece of my puzzle for a little while now. How to get into words what I currently experience in my life. Write it in a way that makes sense and captures my spirit.

I shared a little of my life in the beginning of this book. My early years and into my 20s and 30s just were not that good. And I think that's an understatement. I really struggled. I was in psychological pain I think since the moment I was born, or at least since 5 years old. I remember at 12 years old I recognized that what was happening to me within my immediate family wasn't good. I knew I was messed up. I also knew that it would take me some work to undo what had been done to me. To find some sense of reality.

In my early 20s I was diagnosed with PTSD, depression, anxiety, and a depersonalization disorder. I worked so hard with a psychologist who specialized in PTSD. I really just wanted to feel human. And not live in complete terror. In therapy, we worked on my trauma and how I felt and how skewed reality was for me based on my early experiences. Ok so it was really bad for me.

Now I'm in my 50s and seriously, I simply cannot believe how far I have come. Life is super good. I am doing what I love and loving what I do. But more than that, my emotions and feelings are within my control. I can smile even on a terrible day. My thinking is clear, not muddled anymore through the eyes of a victim.

I am thriving. Let me tell you a little bit of a story, hopefully I can do it justice and convey the message.

Recently I was pulled into a little bit of a psychodrama of someone else's creation. When I realized what had occurred, I was befuddled. The situation dragged me right into old habits and reactions from my childhood. I was hurt, confused, and not sure what to do. My insides told me to just try to hide. Try not to think about it. Just avoid it.

It didn't take long to let my inner adult step up and take charge of me. I knew the feelings were old. But I couldn't get the separation from them that I desperately needed. Of course I hunted my therapist down. I hadn't seen him in a few years and I have to say it took a little work. But it was imperative for me to see someone that knew *ME.*

While I talked through this aggravating trouble I was in, I feel my adult mind kicking into higher gear. And begin to physically feel the old emotions appearing. While we talked, I could then begin to feel the old feelings detaching from my current day reality and melting away. It was like magic. And during that conversation I was completely enchanted at how beautifully the process was working inside me.

For me, thriving is a way of life. I think about sunshine and rainbows and everything good, when the word thrive comes to mind. When I do an internal check of myself, I know my heart is pure. I know my intentions are genuine. I know that when someone is going through something, I simply cannot judge them. My insides don't work that way. Not anymore.

But sometimes even when people are thriving some things in life are still going to be difficult. Ultimately, for me, thriving is about how I move through life. Including all the challenges it brings.

In my not-so-good days, I looked through the eyes of a victim. It was totally natural based on the life from which I came. I approached every aspect of life as a victim and didn't realize it.

After a lot of hard work I now live in gratitude with my heart open and live a commitment to God in every single day.

I have learned so much in my lifetime about the inner workings of me. And now I get to share what I know with others. And for me, that doesn't become a preachy kind of thing. I get to share myself in a way that, hopefully, they will understand and be able to implement it in their own lives.

In my interactions with everyone I meet, I approach them non-judgmentally, with love in my heart and joy for life. My insides are peaceful and when I am talking with another, I think (or hope) it comes through loud and clear.

At the end of the day, in my current life, I live an empowered, self-directed life. I get to make my own choices, choose my own projects, impact others' lives and our county in ways I would never have imagined. I drive the Hope Mobile to give hope away as I drive the streets of our community. I believe in mental health recovery and I believe it is within every person's reach. We are much much more than the place from which we came. I lost a lot of years by not realizing things that I did not know. About emotions, relationships, careers, creating a life and so much more. My life's work is dedicated first to God, and then to help as many people as I can in reaching their personal life goals. I hope that this workbook will reflect my life's work. I hope that it will inspire you to create a life you have always imagined. And even more.

I have a lot of positive saying on the walls of my office. Three are my favorite:

>If you have one friend you hold the hand of the world.
>Shine Bright.
>And my favorite… because I am… simply blessed.

Dear Future Self

Today's Date

....

Instruction

Writing a letter to your future self lets you reflect on your current life, your goals, dreams and values.

Determine how long you want to save this letter before opening it. Seal it in an envelope with "Do not open until _____" on the outside.

Reading it later can show you how much you've grown, what is important to you, and get you back on track, if needed.

Dear me,

_____

_____

_____

_____

_____

_____

_____

_____

_____

_____

_____

_____

_____

_____

_____

Sincerely,

APPENDIX I

Self Care Plan

A self care plan, or safety plan as it's often called, can help you determine what to do when a crisis begins, before it escalates. It would be most helpful to answer the questions when a crisis is not occurring. Please fill out this plan to the extent you are able.

Signs before a crisis begins
What situations, thoughts, images, physical sensations, thinking patterns or behaviors let you know that you need to use your safety plan?

_____

_____

_____

_____

Things I can do to help myself
What can you do to distract yourself from suicidal thoughts when you're alone that help you feel better? Some examples are playing with a pet, reading, playing a game on a computer or your phone, drawing/crafting or exercising.

_____

_____

_____

_____

Positive people and places that can help distract or soothe me

Name: _____   Phone #: _____

Name: _____   Phone #: _____

Name: _____   Phone #: _____

Place: _____

Place: _____

Place: _____

Helpful people:
This could be a supportive person who knows your mental health history and has an idea of what they can do to help you through a crisis. List more than one person, if possible. Who do you feel comfortable and safe talking with when you are in a crisis. Please do not judge yourself if no one comes to mind.

Name: _____   Phone #: _____

Name: _____   Phone #: _____

Name: _____   Phone #: _____

Name: _____   Phone #: _____

Professionals or agencies that provide crisis support:
Please take a few moments to look up your local information to put in this section when you are in a more clear state of mind. It will be easier to reference if or when a crisis arises.

Clinician Name: _____

      Phone #: _____

      Emergency Contact #: _____

Clinician Name: _____

      Phone #: _____

      Emergency Contact #: _____

Suicide Prevention Lifeline: 1-800-273-TALK (8255)

Crisis Text Line: 741741

National Hopeline Network: 1-800-442-HOPE (4673)

Veterans Crisis Line: 1-800-273-8255

Veterans Text Line: 838255

Local hotline: _____

Local Emergency Service: _____

Mental Health Emergency Services Address: _____

Mental Health Emergency Services Phone: _____

Creating a safe environment
Remove things from your home that put you in danger – ask someone to store them for you (Ex. pills, knives, guns, poison, etc.). List the items here.

_____

_____

_____

_____

_____

Who can help you remove items from your home that put you in danger?

_____

_____

_____

_____

_____

List any support groups that you can use or plan to use:

_____

_____

_____

_____

_____

What is most important to you? What gives you hope?

_____

_____

_____

I deserve to live because:

_____

_____

_____

I <u>want</u> to live because:

_____

_____

_____

I choose to live because:

_____

_____

_____

Further thoughts:

_____

_____

_____

_____

_____

_____

_____

_____

APPENDIX II

Resources

Including smartphone apps, online therapy, help lines, crisis lines, and organizations

This list is provided as a convenience to you. You must determine at your sole discretion whether to contact, consult with or utilize the advice or resources. Listing these resources does not constitute an endorsement by Trillium Center, Inc.

Smartphone Applications that may be helpful:
Pixels - Track your mood in a simple, quick and easy manner
Breathe 2 Relax- Free; teaches breathing techniques to manage stress, anxiety disorders, and PTSD
HAPPIFY – May have cost associated; Self guided application aimed to increase positive emotions
Virtual Hope Box - a coping skill app designed for individuals struggling with depression
Mindshift – Free; Helpful for managing symptoms of anxiety and panic attacks
Moodkit - Helps with depression, anxiety, anger management; identify and challenge thought patterns
Moodtools - helps users manage depression through Cognitive Behavioral Therapy (CBT)
T2MoodTracker – Free; for depression, anxiety, stress, trauma related feelings

Professional Mental Health Therapy Online
Talkspace - https://www.talkspace.com/
7 Cups of Tea (aka 7 Cups) - https://www.7cups.com/
Amwell - https://amwell.com/cm/services/online-therapy/
Betterhelp - https://www.betterhelp.com/

> Trillium Team's wish for you:
> **Be strong enough to stand alone.**
> **Smart enough to know when you need help.**
> **And brave enough to ask for it.**

Call a HelpLine for Immediate Support
National Alliance on Mental Illness (NAMI) Helpline - 1-800-950-NAMI (6264) or info@nami.org
Mental Health America (MHA) - Crisis Text Line - Text HOME to 741741

Mental Health Crisis Lines / Suicide Hotlines
Suicide Prevention Lifeline -- 1-800-273-TALK   Crisis Text Line -- Text HOME to 741741
   Online Chat: https://suicidepreventionlifeline.org/chat/
Veterans Crisis Line: 1-800-273-8255, press 1 or text to 838255
   Online chat: https://www.veteranscrisisline.net/get-help/chat
Trevor HelpLine / Suicide Prevention for LGBTQ+ Teens -- 1-866-488-7386
Gay & Lesbian National Hotline -- 1-888-THE-GLNH (1-888-843-4564)
IMAlive -- online crisis chat
National Runaway Safeline -- 1-800-RUNAWAY (chat available on website)
Teenline -- 310-855-4673 Text TEEN to 839863 (teens helping teens)

Organizations
American Association of Suicidology, 202.237.2280, https://suicidology.org/
National Association for Behavioral Healthcare, 202.393.6700, https://www.nabh.org/
National Council for Mental Wellbeing, 202.684.7457, https://www.thenationalcouncil.org
Depression and Bi-Polar Support Alliance, https://www.dbsalliance.org/
National Institute of Mental Health, 866.615.6464, https://www.nimh.nih.gov
American Foundation for Suicide Prevention, 888.333.AFSP (2377), https://www.afsp.org
National Mental Health Consumers' Self-Help Clearinghouse, www.mhselfhelp.org

Still not sure where to get mental health help?
SAMHSA - https://findtreatment.samhsa.gov/
   Enter your zip code to find local resources

If you think

you are broken

Look again.

You are as whole

as your mind

allows you to believe.

So believe.